Sarrasine

Drama Series 15

Paul Tana

Bruno Ramirez

Sarrasine

A Screenplay

Translated from the French,
Italian and Sicilian by Robert Gray

Guernica

Toronto/New York/Lancaster

1996

Original Title: La Sarrasine
Originally published in French by Boréal in 1992.
Copyright © Paul Tana and Bruno Ramirez, 1992, 1996
Translation © Robert Gray and Guernica Editions, 1996.
Afterword © Francesco Loriggio, 1996.
All rights reserved.
Typesetting in Garamond by Calista Del Paese, Toronto.
Printed in Canada.

The Publisher and Translator would like to thank The Canada Council, Le ministère de la
Culture du Québec, and Ontario Arts Council for their support.

Antonio D'Alfonso, Editor.
Guernica Editions Inc.
P.O. Box 117, Station P, Toronto (ON), Canada M5S 2S6
250 Sonwil Drive, Buffalo, N.Y. 14225 U.S.A.
Gazelle, Falcon House, Queen Square, Lancaster LA1 1RN U.K.

National Library of Canada
Library of Congress Catalog Card Number: 95-81764

Canadian Cataloguing in Publication Data
Ramirez, Bruno, 1942-
[Sarrasine. English. 1996]
Sarrasine.
(Drama series ; 15)
Translation of: La Sarrasine published Montréal: Boréal, 1992.
Film script.
ISBN 1-55071-041-9
I. Tana, Paul. II Gray, Robert. III. Title.
IV. Title: Sarrasine. English. 1996. V. Series.
PN1997.S2713 1996 C842'.54 C95-920954-9

Table of Contents

Foreword

At the risk of throwing you off track, before presenting *Sarrasine*, we would like to tell you about fig trees. As you know, these trees grow almost everywhere in the Mediterranean. For many years now, Montreal's Italian immigrants have also succeeded in growing fig trees in their gardens. The fig is a delicate tree, and to help it survive the rigours of the Quebec winter, they have devised a strategy. Every autumn around the month of November they uproot the trees, lay them in a trench and cover them with straw and earth. When spring comes, they dig them up, the leaves grow again and, come summer, the trees bear fruit... Just before the first frost, the cycle begins anew.

For the Italians of Quebec, growing fig trees is one way of appropriating a country which is still not entirely their own, of taking possession of this land, to a certain extent, by transplanting something familiar to them from their first culture, their past. In so doing, they transform this country as well as themselves...

With our *Sarrasine*, we, like them, have sought to appropriate a piece of this country; we have done so by telling a story. Our story grew out of a newspaper account of a universe that rarely surfaces in the collective memory of the

Quebecois: the universe of immigrants. In Montreal, at the beginning of the century, an Italian accidentally shot and killed a French Canadian. For this he was sentenced to death. The judge had intended to set an example; he wished to discipline those foreigners who had the regrettable habit of carrying weapons and taking justice into their own hands.

By exploring this simple news item, we wanted to do more than simply tell a tale of injustice against the backdrop of the absurd logic of everyday racism and violence. We wanted to relate the story of characters who, strangely, because of the play of chance and destiny, always find themselves somewhere else than where they want to be. This 'other' place may be our country, a product of the two cultures that created us.

So, instead of planting a fig tree, we have summoned up characters in places and landscapes where they have always been invisible; we have contrasted their Sicilian dialect with the language of Quebec; we have soiled ever so slightly the whiteness of the Quebec winter by placing on it, at the end of the film, the figure of Ninetta Moschella — a black stain on the snow... hers and ours.

Paul Tana and Bruno Ramirez

Main Cast and Crew

Alphonse Lamoureux: Jean Lapointe

Félicité Lemieux: Johanne-Marie Tremblay

Melo Ingrassia: Frank Crudell

Pasquale Lopinto: Gaetano Cisco Cimarosa

Ninetta Moschella: Enrica Maria Modugno

Giuseppe Moschella: Tony Nardi

Carmelo: Nick La Morgia

Joe Ingrassia: Domenico Fiore

Priest: Jacques Rossi

Margie Dubois: Murielle Dutil

Théo Lemieux: Gilbert Sicotte

Adrien: Luc Picard

Father Phaneuf: André Brassard

Judge: Yvon Charette

Mr. Saint-Louis: Robert Lalonde

Celi: Nelson Villagra

Salvatore Moschella: Biagio Pelligra

Angelo Di Biasi: Vincenzo Ierfino

SARRASINE

Mr. Thompson: Len Watt

Pietro Fochera: Salvatore Sciascia

Otello: Roger Michael

Langelier: Paul Savoie

Mr. LeBlanc: Alain Fournier

Cinematographer: Michel Caron

Art Director: François Séguin

Costume Designer: François Barbeau

Editor: Louise Surprenant

Sound Editor: Claude Langlois

Music: Pierre Desrochers

Line Producer: Lise Abastado

Associate Producer: Doris Girard

Producer: Marc Daigle

Written by Paul Tana and Bruno Ramirez

Director: Paul Tana

Note: Lines spoken in Italian or Sicilian in the film appear between brackets immediately below their English translation.

Montreal, 1904.
Alphonse's store. Interior. Day.

The store is almost empty. Only a few pieces of furniture, some boxes and a couch remain.

Alphonse Lemieux stands at the store window, gazing at the street. A wagon goes by. He turns, surveying the room.

From his desk in a corner of the store he picks up a photograph of himself standing in front of the Eiffel Tower. He smiles, bemused.

Alphonse's room. Interior. Day.

Félicité Lemieux is packing her father's trousers and sweaters into a large trunk. Beside her on the bed lie various objects (books, a reproduction of the Discobulus, *patent leather boots). Shirts and other personal belongings are piled on the dressing table behind her.*

Alphonse comes in, carrying the photograph from the previous scene. He pats his daughter on the shoulder as he goes by, lays the portrait on the bed, and removes from the wall a photograph of a woman. He admires it for a few seconds, then hands it to Félicité.

ALPHONSE

Here, pack this, too.

Félicité takes the portrait and dusts if with the cuff of her dress.

FÉLICITÉ

No! This stays here. It's the only picture of Maman I have, and I want to keep it.

ALPHONSE

With a wry smile.

It's true that Margie might not appreciate it!

FÉLICITÉ

Also smiling.

Well, if I were her, I wouldn't either!

She packs the photograph of Alphonse in the trunk, then, with a fond look, pretends to scold him.

FÉLICITÉ

Your ladies!

Alphonse glances at his watch.

ALPHONSE

I have to be going. Don't forget to pack my bathrobe. Even if it is old...

Félicité laughs, sharing the joke. He leaves.

Street. Exterior. Day.

Alphonse steps out of his store on his way to the tailor's.

Giuseppe Moschella's workroom.
Interior. Day.

A makeshift puppet theatre has been set up in the workroom. A backdrop representing a medieval castle serves as the set. The two puppeteers (who remain invisible) are Giuseppe and Carmelo.

In the dim light, the spectators – some fifteen Italian immigrants – are shouting, gesticulating and applauding the hero of this episode from Tasso's Jerusalem Delivered. A close-up of the small stage shows Tancred, the Christian, duelling fiercely with Clorinda, the Saracen, in a clash of helmets, swords and shields. Among the men sitting in the first row are Pasquale Lopinto and Melo Ingrassia.

MELO

Get them, Christians!

[Viva li cristiani!]

SPECTATOR

Kill the Saracens!

[A morte li saracini!]

ANOTHER SPECTATOR

Cut off his head!

[Tagliaci la testa!]

PASQUALE

Long live Garibaldi!

[Viva Garibaldi!]

Melo, seated beside Pasquale, looks at him uncomprehendingly.

MELO

What's Garibaldi got to do with it?

[Ma che c'entra Garibaldi?]

PASQUALE

Mind your own business!

[Fatti i cazzi tuoi!]

Moschella's kitchen. Interior. Day.

At the kitchen table, Ninetta Moschella is copying in her notebook sentences from an Italian grammar. She forms the letters awkwardly: she is learning to write.

Noises and voices from the workroom are heard off-screen.

Kitchen/Front hall. Interior. Day.

The vestibule door opens and Alphonse Lamoureux walks in. He takes a few steps toward the workroom, then stops, as if reluctant to disturb. Ninetta sees him and rises to greet him.

NINETTA

Hello, monsieur Alphonse.

ALPHONSE

Hello.

NINETTA

Smiling, in a low voice.

Come in, monsieur Alphonse. It won't be long.

She leads him toward the workroom.

Workroom. Interior. Day.

Ninetta and Alphonse make their way through the crowd of excited spectators.

ALPHONSE

Indicating the theatre.

It's wonderful.

NINETTA

Shouting to make herself heard above the din.

My husband loves his puppets. That's Tancred, the Christian. He's going to kill the Saracen. He doesn't know that the Saracen is Clorinda, the woman he loves.

Alphonse nods. Giuseppe's voice brings silence to the room.

GIUSEPPE

'At the first rays of dawn, after a night of combat, the two warriors pause.'

['Alle prime luci dell'alba, i due guerrieri che hanno combattuto tutta la notte si fermano.']

GIUSEPPE

Playing Tancred.

'Tell me your name, I pray. Thus, whether victorious or vanquished, I may know to whom I owe victory or death.'

['Ti prego, svelami il tuo nome acciò ch'io sappia, o vinto o vincitore, chi la mia morte o la vittoria onore.']

CARMELO

Playing Clorinda.

'You ask in vain. It is not my wont to reveal my name. But know that I was one of the pair who set fire to the tower.'

['Invano chiedi, non è mio uso rivelar il mio nome; sono uno dei due che incendiò la torre.']

GIUSEPPE

Playing Tancred.

'Your words and your silence, o insolent barbarian, incite me to vengeance!'

['Le tue parole come il tuo silenzio, o barbaro discortese, mi incitano alla vendetta.']

> *On stage, the two knights resume combat. The spectators take up their shouts of encouragement. Suddenly, Tancred deals a fatal blow to his adversary, and the Saracen collapses.*

PASQUALE

> *Getting carried away. Yelling at Clorinda, on stage.*

There! Take that, you whore!

[Te lo meritavi! Puttana!]

Several men applaud.

MELO

Shut up, you idiot!

[Ma statte zitto, ignorante!]

PASQUALE

Indignant.

Why'd she stick her nose in men's business?

[Ma picchi s'intriga nè cosi de masculi?]

On stage, Clorinda is dying.

CARMELO

Playing Clorinda.

'Friend, you have won. I forgive you. Baptize me and cleanse me of my sins.'

['Amico hai vinto, io ti perdono, dammi il battesimo ch'ogni mia colpa lava.']

Ninetta and Alphonse exchange a smile.

GIUSEPPE

Continuing the narration.

'Deeply moved, Tancred goes to a nearby stream and fills his helmet with water.'

['Tancredi commosso si reca nel vicino ruscello e riempie il suo elmo d'acqua.']

The workroom is again plunged in intense silence, the drama reflected in the faces of the spectators.

GIUSEPPE

'Clorinda raises her visor, revealing her face. Tancred recognizes his beloved.'

['Clorinda alza la visiera scoprendo il viso. Tancredi vede e riconosce in lei la donna da lui amata.']

Clorinda, lying on the ground, lifts her visor.

GIUSEPPE

'Distraught, he tries to save her, but in vain.'

['E dal dolor affranto invano cerca di ricondurla in vita.']

An angel descends over Clorinda. The spectators gasp in amazement.

CARMELO

Playing Clorinda.

'The heavens open. I go in peace.'

['S'apre il ciel, io vado in pace.']

The angel moves as if to take Clorinda's soul, then flies up and disappears. A woman spectator wipes away her tears, to the mocking amusement of her husband.

GIUSEPPE

'Weep, Tancred. You will pay for every drop of blood with a sea of tears.'

['Piangi, o Tancredi, gli occhi tuoi pagheran di quel sangue ogni stilla un mar di pianto.']

Enthusiastic applause greets these final words. The curtain falls.

'Bravi! Bravissimi!'

Workroom. Interior. Day.

A little later.

Melo, Joe and Pasquale are straightening up the room. Alphonse walks over to Giuseppe and shakes his hand.

ALPHONSE

You're a man of many talents, monsieur Moschella.

The two men walk toward the small stage.

GIUSEPPE

A little fun on Sunday...

He puts his hand on Alphonse's shoulder.

So tomorrow's the big day, monsieur Lamoureux?

ALPHONSE

Yes, it is. Yes, it is.

Alphonse indicates the puppets with his hand.

GIUSEPPE

These two have followed me everywhere since I left Sicily.

Taking one of the puppets.

This is Clorinda.

He hands it to Carmelo.

Carmelo, get monsieur Lamoureux's suit.

To Alphonse.

Wait till you see what we've done for you! Come with me.

They walk off-camera. The boarders continue to clean up the workroom.

Moschella's workroom. Interior. Day.

Later. Carmelo is adjusting the wings of a full-length mirror. In the background we see Melo, Joe and Pasquale playing cards. Alphonse walks into the foreground wearing a new pair of trousers and a vest. Giuseppe smiles with pride.

GIUSEPPE

Step up to the mirror.

Alphonse obeys. Carmelo brings over the jacket that completes the suit.

GIUSEPPE

I'll take it, Carmelo.

[Gira, Carmelo.]

Giuseppe takes the jacket and helps Alphonse put it on.

Fits like a glove!

With expert hands, he smooths the jacket so it falls just right.

Your bride will be proud of you!

ALPHONSE

Smiling.

Yes.

Giuseppe opens the jacket to show off his handiwork.

GIUSEPPE

Look at the finishing!

ALPHONSE

Lovely.

GIUSEPPE

Adjusting the jacket.

A young man!

The two men laugh.

ALPHONSE

Perfect! I'm telling you, monsieur Moschella, you have a great future ahead of you in Montreal.

Alphonse takes a few more steps toward the mirror and admires himself with satisfaction. His gaze darkens as he looks at the trousers.

GIUSEPPE

Is something wrong?

ALPHONSE

Here, look. Is there a tuck in the trousers?

GIUSEPPE

No. Carmelo!

Joking.

You know, monsieur Lamoureux, it's not the pants that matter, but what's in them! We'll fix it for you.

Giuseppe stoops to adjust the trousers. Seated around the table at a game of cards, the boarders observe the scene with amusement.

CARMELO

Speriamo que domani, u signuri cià fa nchianari...

The three men break into laughter. Giuseppe gets to his feet, sharing the joke. Alphonse turns to look at the boarders.

ALPHONSE

Smiling.

What did he say?

GIUSEPPE

Laughing.

He hopes that tomorrow, the good Lord will help you raise your mast.

Alphonse laughs good-naturedly and leans to whisper in Giuseppe's ear.

ALPHONSE

Me, too!

They both laugh. Then, out loud.

I'll let you know.

Another burst of laughter.

Ninetta comes over carrying a tray with a decanter, glasses and a cake. She gestures to Giuseppe, who leads his client to the table.

GIUSEPPE

Come here. You're going to taste something special.

Around the table in the workroom.
Interior. Day.

Ninetta places the tray on the table and offers Alphonse a piece of cake.

NINETTA

Would you like some?

ALPHONSE

Thank you... It's good! Did you make it?

Ninetta nods with a smile, then offers cake to the boarders, who are still deep in their card game.

GIUSEPPE

It's a cake from back home: *pignolata.*

NINETTA

Excuse me...

She is about to leave. Giuseppe catches her and kisses her hand. She goes.

GIUSEPPE

Monsieur Lamoureux, I would like to drink to your marriage and your new life in St. Zénon.

As he talks, Giuseppe fills the glasses and hands one to Alphonse. The boarders follow this conversation with interest.

And let me say that Montreal won't be the same without you.

JOE

Well spoken, don Giuseppe, well spoken!

[Ben detto, don Giuseppe, ben detto!]

With a smile, Giuseppe pushes the tray and glasses toward the boarders.

ALPHONSE

As you know, the wedding is for family only, but I wish you'd come to our reception. How can I convince you?

GIUSEPPE

You cannot, monsieur Alphonse. I'd prefer to respect your privacy. That's how I am.

Jocular.

I won't be there, but I'll be thinking of you.

Alphonse raises his glass.

ALPHONSE

To our friendship, Giuseppe. I want you to know you're my favourite Italian. After Garibaldi, of course.

PASQUALE

In English.

Hey, Mister, you know Garibaldi?

ALPHONSE

In English.

Sure, I was in Caprera. I put flowers on the grave of the great man.

PASQUALE

You don't say!

[Minchia!]

GIUSEPPE

Chiding him.

Pasquale, monsieur Lamoureux has travelled the world!

ALPHONSE

What's more, he gave you a country.

GIUSEPPE

No, no, no! He was the spark, monsieur Lamoureux, but Sicily was the flame of Italy's unification!

ALPHONSE

To Sicily!

GIUSEPPE

To your marriage!

Church square. Exterior. Day.

It is early morning. Carmelo in the lead, Pasquale pushes his barrel organ toward the entrance of the church.

CARMELO

In Canada, the older and the uglier you are, the earlier in the morning you get married. So no one sees! Smart, huh?

[O Canada cosi è: più brutto e vecchio sei, più ti sposi presto la mattina quando nessuno ti vede. Smart, ei!]

PASQUALE

They want to be alone, so why barge in with our bloody music?

[Ma scusa, quelli vogliono rimanere soli, e spuntiamo noi con 'sto cazzo di serenata?]

CARMELO

Come on, Pasquale, you know how don Peppe is. He gets these ideas sometimes. What can you do?

[Dai, Pasquale, tu sai com'è don Peppe, certe volte ha le idee un pò strano, che ci vuoi fare?]

PASQUALE

With my ugly mug, think I could get married here?

[Allora iu na 'stu paese co sta faccia non mi marito qui?]

CARMELO

Married, what do you mean? You have four kids in Italy!

[Ma che maritare! Pensa ai tuoi quattro figli in Italia.]

PASQUALE

Shut your face, idiot.

[Statte zitto, cretino]

Church. Interior. Day.

We see the faces of Pasquale and Carmelo through the windows of the main doors of the church. They stand there for a minute, watching the ceremony. Into this subdued atmosphere, the priest enters, accompanied by organ music. He kneels before the altar. We see Alphonse and Margie, who is sitting in a wheelchair.

Pasquale and Carmelo take off their hats and enter the church. Carmelo crosses himself.

PRIEST

Marguerite Dubois and Alphonse Lamoureux, you have come here today to enter the holy bonds of matrimony.

PASQUALE

Appalled.

Carmelo, did you see the bride?

[Carmelo l'hai vista, la sposa?]

The priest adresses Alphonse and Margie.

PRIEST

...pledge fidelity and support, in sickness and in health, till death do you part.

In the back of the church, Carmelo has moved closer to Pasquale.

CARMELO

Whispering.

She was his first love. But he went to sea, so she moved to Lowell, in the States, and got married there. They didn't see each other for years. Her husband died two years ago. And now, in their old age, they've found each other again. The Frenchman told don Peppe the story.

[È stato il suo primo amore. Poi, lui si è imbarcato e lei se n'è andata a Lowell, in America, e s'è fatta la famiglia... E non si sono visti più. Suo marito è morto due anni fa... E ora, nella vecchiaia, si so rimessi insieme. È il francese che l'ha raccontato a don Peppe...]

PASQUALE

Moved.

Ah, destiny!

[O vedi il destino, ei!]

At the altar, the ceremony continues.

MARGIE

I do.

PRIEST

Alphonse Lamoureux, do you take to be your wife, Marguerite Dubois, here present, in accordance with the rituals of our holy mother Church?

ALPHONSE

I do.

PRIEST

Take her right hand.

Hearing these words, Pasquale decides that the time has come.

PASQUALE

Turning on his heels.

Now for the music!

[Cca ci vuole la musica!]

CARMELO

Trying to stop him.

No, not yet!

[No, ancora no!]

PASQUALE

Leaving.

I know what I'm supposed to do.

[Io u saccio chiddu chi fazzu.]

Church square. Exterior. Day.

Pasquale walks quickly out of the church, with Carmelo trailing.

CARMELO

But don Peppe said the music was for when they come out!

[Ma don Giuseppe ci ha detto che la musica è per quando escono!]

Pasquale vigorously cranks his organ.

PASQUALE

Shut up. I know what I'm doing.

[Statte muto, lo so io quello che fazzo.]

He sets the machine in gear and music begins to play. Pasquale opens wide the doors of the church and walks inside. Music fills the nave. Surprised faces turn back to the entrance, where Pasquale and Carmelo appear. Pasquale takes a few steps back and forth, hands behind his back, obviously proud of what he has done.

We see Léon in profile, his face flushed with irritation. Félicité turns Rita's face away from the scene. Félicité looks at Théo. Outraged, Théo finally stands up and strides toward the back of the church. Motioning broadly, he orders Pasquale and Carmelo to leave.

THÉO

Get out of here! Get out! Get out! Move it!

Church square. Exterior. Day.

Outside, the music continues. Théo closes the church doors behind him.

THÉO

Will you stop that goddamn music! Well?

CARMELO

It's monsieur Giuseppe's wedding present.

THÉO

Did you hear what I said? I want you to turn that off and get the hell out of here, both of you!

CARMELO

But we can't turn it off.

THÉO

Why not?

CARMELO

Pasquale, you explain to him.

THÉO

Then I'll turn it off! I'll show you!

Théo races to the barrel organ, shakes the crank, then siezes the wagon by the handles to push it away. Pasquale leaps at him.

PASQUALE

Shouting in English.

Hey! Don't touch my music!

He reaches for his knife and grabs Théo. In the ensuing scuffle, Théo, surprised by this unexpected attack, attempts to overpower Pasquale and hold the hand with the knife.

THÉO

Shouting.

Hey! Hey! Hey!

PASQUALE

In English.

I told you, don't touch my music.

In Italian.

Touch it and I'll kill you!

[Non toccare, ma io t'amazzo, sai!]

Pasquale slashes Théo's hand with his knife. Théo lets out a scream and doubles over in pain.

Carmelo pulls Pasquale by the shoulders, trying to lead him away.

CARMELO

C'mon!

[Iamocenne!]

PASQUALE

Straining to break free.

Let go of me!

[E lassame!]

CARMELO

That's enough, Pasquale, c'mon!

[Basta, Pasquale, iamocenne!]

Théo stands up, examines his wound and takes a handkerchief from his pocket to staunch the blood. He watches Carmelo and Pasquale hurry off with the organ.

PASQUALE

Turning back to Théo, in English.

Next time your face!

CARMELO

Pasquale!

THÉO

Shouting, in English.

Any time!

PASQUALE

That son of a bitch!

[Ma guarda 'sto stronzo!]

Church. Interior. Day.

The wedding ceremony is over. Théo enters the church, the handkerchief tied around his hand. Alphonse walks over to meet him.

ALPHONSE

Furious, in a low voice.

Proud of yourself?

THÉO

Whispering, indignant.

Disturbing us like that! Did you see what they did to me?

ALPHONSE

They weren't disturbing me.

THÉO

Raising his voice.

You're taking their side now?

ALPHONSE

They didn't know any better.

THÉO

They'll learn their place. This is Canada, monsieur Lamoureux, not Sicily!

Alphonse spins around before Théo can finish his sentence. Félicité appears.

FÉLICITÉ

Stop it!

She bends over to examine Théo's wound.

Front hall of Moschella's house.
Interior. Day.

In the kitchen, in the background, Ninetta is sorting the dirty laundry. We hear Giuseppe berating Pasquale and Carmelo.

GIUSEPPE

I sent you to take a gift, not to fight like dogs!

[Vi mandai per portare un regalo, e no per azzuffarvi come dei cani.]

Pasquale comes out of the workroom into the hallway.

PASQUALE

But I told you, Peppe, he wouldn't listen! The sonofabitch was ready to bust my organ. What should I have done?

[Ma tu dissi, Peppe: quello non vulia sentiri nenti; il solo interesse di stu figghiu di puttana è di scassarmi ù pianino! Che potevo fare?]

Giuseppe follows him into the hallway.

GIUSEPPE

Anything except pull out your knife.

[Qualunque cosa, tranne di usciri il coltello!]

PASQUALE

Gesturing toward his crotch.

Then pull out what, this maybe?

[E chi ci avia a nesciri, chistu?]

Giuseppe hesitates for a few seconds before answering with a hint of contempt.

GIUSEPPE

Not a bad idea. You would've caused less harm.

[Non sarebbe stata na mala cosa... Anzi, avresti creato meno problemi!]

Pasquale doesn't know how to answer, unsure if Giuseppe is joking. But Giuseppe continues, sternly.

GIUSEPPE

Your head, Pasquale! When will you learn to use it? You know that Alphonse isn't simply a client, he's a friend. Even if the Frenchman was in the wrong, a knife wouldn't settle anything.

[A testa, Pasquale, a testa! Quando imparerai a usarla! Tu scurdasti che Alphonse è più che un cliente, è un amico! Anche si u francisi s'é comportato male, non è col coltello che si sistemano ste cose, unni semo?]

PASQUALE

Stubborn.

Knife or no knife, that was for me to decide. He asked for it. It was his fault.

[Senti, si pigghiu u cuteddu o no su affari mei! Anche se se lo meritava. La colpa è sua.]

GIUSEPPE

Losing his temper.

God in heaven! It was your fault! The music was for when Alphonse came out of the church. But no, you always have to do things your way! You're nothing but a hoodlum, Pasquale, a hoodlum.

[Porco Giuda! È colpa tua. Perché la musica era per quando Alphonse usciva dalla chiesa. Invece no; per forza hai fatto di testa tua come al solito. Sei peggio de no zingaro, Pasquale, peggio.]

PASQUALE

Exasperated.

That's easy for you to say. But what would you have done in my shoes? Besides, it was your fault! They wanted to be left alone, in peace. But you sent me with that damn music! Ah, Peppe!

[È facile chiachierare, sai, è facile, vorrei vedere a tia al posto mio. E poi la colpa è tua, Peppe, perché quelli dovevano stare in pace, nell'intimo, e mi mandi a mia, co' sto cazzo di pian-ino! Ah, Peppe!]

He walks out, slamming the door behind him. Giuseppe is shaken by Pasquale's last words. He takes his overcoat off a hook and tosses it over his arm.

NINETTA

Where are you going, Giuseppe?

[Unni vai a stura, Giuseppe?]

Giuseppe turns to face her, then walks off, without answering. Carmelo appears in the hall.

GIUSEPPE

To Carmelo.

And you?

[E tu?]

Carmelo lowers his head, ashamed. Giuseppe leaves.

Chez Lavoie Tavern. Interior. Day.

Cyrille Lavoie, the tavern's owner, is leaning against the bar, reading a newspaper. In the mirror behind Cyrille, we see Giuseppe, who is having a drink at the bar. We can also see a part of the front window as well as two other clients.

After a few seconds, Lavoie looks up and speaks to Giuseppe.

LAVOIE

Ironic.

Hey, Moschella! There's more about you guys. Listen here: 'From Sing Sing to Montreal: U.S. authorities are convinced that Italian gangster Vincenzo Romita, who escaped from Sing Sing Penitentiary three days ago, is hiding in Montreal, where he lived a few years ago. He is considered armed and dangerous.'

Giuseppe is obviously irritated by what he hears.

LAVOIE

Teasing.

Is he staying with you?

Lavoie turns around and picks up a bottle. Giuseppe takes a few coins from his pocket and throws them on the counter.

GIUSEPPE

Peeved.

Dumb bastard!

[Ignorante di merda.]

He walks to the door. Lavoie protests good-heartedly.

LAVOIE

Moschella, I didn't mean any harm.

Giuseppe slams the door behind him.

Covered passage. Exterior. Day.

Giuseppe hurries away. He walks by a newspaper vendor, then, thinking it over, turns and calls to the vendor and buys a paper. He glances at the headlines, then continues on his way.

Moschella's workroom. Interior. Night.

GIUSEPPE

They clash with helmets...

[Cozzan con gli elmi...]

NINETTA

Wait!

[Aspetta...]

Ninetta writes, then Giuseppe goes on.

GIUSEPPE

They clash with helmets and swords...

[Cozzan con gli elmi insieme e con gli scudi...]

Ninetta hesitates, unsure how to spell one of the words. Giuseppe goes over to her and reads over her shoulder.

GIUSEPPE

'Sword' with a 'd', not 'swort'. 'Clash'... with an 'sh'... 'Clash!'

['Scudi'... 'scudi' con la 'd', non con la 't'... 'Cozzan'... con due zeta... 'Cozzan!']

NINETTA

Vexed.

Couldn't you dictate something easier?

[Non mi potevi dettare una cosa più facile!]

GIUSEPPE

Do you want to learn to write, yes or no?

[Vuoi imparare a scrivere, sì o no?]

NINETTA

Shh, everyone's sleeping!

[Chut... ! Svegli a tutti!]

GIUSEPPE

Lowering his voice.

Go on, write! 'Three times the knight embraces her in his mighty arms, and three times again... '

[Dai, dai, scrivi: 'Tre volte il cavalier la donna stringe... Con le robuste braccia ed altrettante poi...']

Giuseppe starts to dictate much too quickly again.

NINETTA

Wait, I asked you to go slower!

[Aspetta, ti dissi più piano...]

But Giuseppe, inspired by Tasso's poetry, pays no attention and reads on as before. Ninetta angrily lays down her pen.

GIUSEPPE

'Three times the knight embraces her. Three times she escapes from his iron grasp – an enemy's grasp, not a lover's. Crossing swords, each, in turn, draws blood. Exhausted and panting, they finally withdraw to catch their breath.'

['Tre volte il cavalier la donna stringe. Da qui nodi tenaci ella si scinge. Nodi di fier nemico, e non d'amante. Tornano al ferro e l'uno e l'altro intinge con molte piaghe e stanco e anelante e questi e quelli al fin pur si ritira e dopo lungo fatica respira.']

Melo appears in the doorway and looks on with fascination as Giuseppe recites the poetry. Giuseppe sees him and abruptly stops.

GIUSEPPE

What do you want?

[Che vuoi?]

MELO

Embarrassed.

Sorry, don Peppe. I forgot to tell you that the Frenchman was here today.

[Scusate, don Peppe, me so scurdato a dicere che oggi è venuto il francese.]

GIUSEPPE

Surprised.

Lamoureux? What did he want?

[Come u francisi... ? che voleva?]

MELO

Hesitant.

I was all alone. There was no one else.

[Stavo solo solo... Non ci stava niscuono...]

GIUSEPPE

Impatient.

What did he say to you?

[Ma cosa ti ha detto?]

MELO

Something about music, the church, St. Zénon... I didn't understand.

[Bo... Parlava di musica, di chiesa, di St. Zénon... No, ho capito bonu.]

GIUSEPPE

Angry.

What do you mean, you didn't understand?

[Come nu capisti, dai?]

MELO

It isn't my fault!

[E chi ci pozzu fari!]

GIUSEPPE

To himself.

These people! He's been in Canada for two years and he still can't speak a word of French!

To Melo.

What are you waiting for?

[Che razza di gente! Dopo due anni di Canada manco una parola di francese sapi spiccicare! Che fai là impalato?]

MELO

All right, I'll go to bed. Good night, don Peppe.

[Va be... Me ne vo a cuccà. Buona notte, don Peppe.]

GIUSEPPE

Good night!

[Buona notte!]

Melo leaves. The news has upset Giuseppe.

GIUSEPPE

To Ninetta.

Did you know that Lamoureux was here?

[Tu sapevi sta storia che Lamoureux è venuto?]

NINETTA

Putting away her books.

No...

GIUSEPPE

Where were you?

[Unni eri tu?]

NINETTA

I don't know!

[Che ni saccio!]

GIUSEPPE

What do you mean, you don't know? Where were you?

[Come 'che ne saccio'? Unni eri?]

NINETTA

A trace of irritation in her voice.

Where do you think I was? At the market.

Getting up.

Your boarders have to eat. Tell Celi to stop sending them. He sent two more more this morning.

[Unni putia esseri? A fari a spisa, no? Deve mangiare la tua ganga di bordanti? Dicci a sto Celi che non me mandasse più gente. Oggi me ne ha mandati altri due...]

GIUSEPPE

Did you send them away?

[E tu che facesti? Li mandasti via?]

NINETTA

Of course! I've already four men to feed, besides you.

Raising her voice.

What do you think I am, an innkeeper?

[Proprio così. Cca ci sono già quattro omini senza contare a tia. Per chi mi pigliasti? Per na locandiera?]

Ninetta leaves the room and starts up the stairs.

GIUSEPPE

Following her, yelling.

Don't send anyone away again. I make the decisions here! Understand?

[La prossima volta tu non mandi via nessuno, sono io che decido ste cose! Va bene?]

Ninetta doesn't answer.

Bedroom in Moschella's house.
Interior. Night.

A bit later.

Ninetta, wearing a nightgown, is brushing her hair in front of the mirror at her dressing table. Giuseppe, in pyjamas, watches her, searching for a way to make peace. He goes over to her and strokes her hair. Ninetta yanks her hair away. Giuseppe tries to take her in his arms, but she pulls away.

NINETTA

Leave me alone!

[Lasciami stare.]

She goes to a corner of the room and lights two candles under a picture of the Virgin, then crosses herself and says a short prayer.

When she steps to the bed to pull back the covers, Giuseppe has a doll in his hands.

GIUSEPPE

What I really want are children, not boarders.

[Certo, saria meglio avere bambini inveci di bordanti.]

NINETTA

Annoyed.

Don't start that again. You know why we don't have any.

[Non ricominicamo con sto discorso. Lo sai perché non abbiami figli.]

GIUSEPPE

So it's my fault? Is it my fault?

[È colpa mia? È colpa mia?]

Without answering, Ninetta takes the doll and puts it away, then sits on the bed to pull off her slippers.

GIUSEPPE

All right, it's my fault. Fine, I'll cut it off!

[Va bene, è colpa mia, no? Vedi che me la taglio!]

Ninetta slips silently under the blankets and turns her back.

NINETTA

Good night.

[Buona notte.]

Giuseppe gets up and leaves. Curious, Ninetta sits up to try to see what he's doing. But as soon as she hears his steps, she lays her head on the pillow and closes her eyes.

GIUSEPPE

I'll cut it off! I'll cut it off!

[Me la taglio! Me la taglio!]

Giuseppe sticks a pair of scissors into his pyjama pants. He snips away, then begins to scream in pain. Despite herself, Ninetta shudders.

NINETTA

Cut off your tongue instead!

[Tagliati piuttosto sta linguaccia!]

She lays her head on the pillow, but her anger has abated.

GIUSEPPE

Okay, my tongue too!

[E va bene, via pure la lingua!]

Giuseppe now pretends to cut off his tongue. Ninetta, who is secretly watching him, smiles. With his left hand, he pretends to take out his tongue; he climbs on the bed and holds it out to Ninetta. She laughs and bites his hand.

GIUSEPPE

Screaming.

Ow, you hurt me!

[Ahi! Ahi! che mi fai male.]

Pretending to be mute, Giuseppe cries out, in pain, then falls silent. They embrace, laughing softly.

Melo's room at Moschella's house.
Interior. Night.

Melo, in pyjamas, is sitting on the edge of his bed, polishing his shoes. He hears muffled laughter, then Ninetta's voice.

NINETTA

I thought you cut it off.

[Non te la tagliasti?]

He smiles, stops for a moment to listen, then energetically resumes brushing his shoes in time with the rhythmic squeaking of the bedsprings in the master bedroom above.

Alphonse Lamoureux's store.
Exterior. Night.

Two ladders are propped against the façade of Alphonse's store, one on each side of the window. Isidore Duchesne, the sign-painter, stands on one of them. A new sign has just been put up: Théodore Lemieux, Greengrocer. *Théo and Rita come out of the store.*

THÉO

To Adrien.

Come on, off with it!

To Rita.

It's nice, huh? Look!

Théo enthusiastically raises his little girl in his arms so she can admire the sign.

Look, that's Daddy.

He spins around, making a circular gesture with his hand.

You see, everyone will come here to buy.

In English, to the sign- painter.

Fine, fine.

In the meantime, Adrien has been scraping off the old lettering on the window: Alphonse Lamoureux, Used Furniture.

Lavoie's tavern. Interior. Night.

The tavern is busy and crowded with clients. The sound of music, glasses knocking together, laughter and joking. Feeling their liquor, men lean against the walls or sit at tables, smoking and shouting happily at each other. In this commotion, Théo — also somewhat drunk — is handing out his business cards.

FIRST CLIENT

Hey, Théo, think you're some kind of lawyer?

THÉO

Laughing.

Not a lawyer, a *businessman.*

SECOND CLIENT

He deals in spuds!

THÉO

Stuffing a card into his coat pocket.

You eat spuds, I'll eat steak! 'Théo Lemieux, Greengrocer.' Each card is a client. That's the modern approach! The sign's already up.

To another prospect.

Here!

ISIDORE

Don't forget to pay me, Théo!

THÉO

To Isidore, who is leaning against the counter.

Hey, in a week your sign'll be paid ten times, a hundred times over, and everyone will know it!

As he says this, Théo sends him on with a slap on the shoulder. He jumps up, sits on the counter, and pours himself a glassful.

FRIEND

Hey, Théo, is the American bride backing you?

THÉO

None of your business, okay?

FRIEND

C'mon, Théo, tell us.

At this moment, Pasquale walks in and heads to the bar.

THÉO

You're jealous, that's all!

Laughter.

FRIEND

A toast to Théo, the businessman!

Lavoie watches as Pasquale unties his bandanna, then pours him a shot.

LAVOIE

You had a good haul today, huh, Pasquale?

Pasquale waves his hand modestly, then raises his glass to Lavoie and empties it in a single gulp.

THÉO

A toast to my father-in-law, who finally decided to quit wasting his time with his old junk and make room for the young!

Pasquale and Lavoie turn automatically toward Théo. Pasquale, recognizing him, is worried.

PASQUALE

To Lavoie, in English.

Hurry up!

But Lavoie is counting Pasquale's coins and gestures to Pasquale to be patient.

THÉO

With a mocking smile.

And to the lovely Margie!

Laughter. Théo glances in the direction of Lavoie and notices Pasquale. His face darkens.

THÉO

Hey, macaroni, what are you doing here? Macaroni, I'm talking to you!

He whistles. Pasquale is careful not to turn toward Théo. He anxiously waits for his money so he can leave.

THÉO

Showing his bandaged hand.

Hey, do you remember this? C'mon, look. Don't be scared!

Théo jumps off the counter and walks over to Pasquale. Adrien and Isidore follow him.

THÉO

Hey, have a drink with us, it's on me tonight!

ALPHONSE

Careful, Théo, he'll cut your other hand!

Pasquale decides to escape without waiting for his money, but Théo grabs him by the collar. Adrien and Isidore each hold him by an arm.

Silence falls over the tavern. The other customers draw round in a circle to watch.

THÉO

Don't leave now. Where's your knife? Show it to my pals.

Théo steps up to search him. Pasquale struggles to get free.

PASQUALE

Let go, you pile of shit!

[Ah! lassame, uomo di merda!]

The three men shove him against the counter. Glasses and bottles topple over noisily. Lavoie protests.

LAVOIE

That's enough, Théo, leave him alone.

THÉO

Searching Pasquale's pockets.

C'mon, where's your knife? Huh? Where'd you put it? Where is it? Don't you have it?

Théo puts a glass in front of Pasquale and fills it.

THÉO

See, Lavoie, I'm giving him a drink. He's such a hard worker, he deserves it!

Laughter.

PASQUALE

In English.

Leave me alone!

Lavoie steps in again and hands Pasquale his money.

LAVOIE

Let him go! Here, Pasquale, go home.

Théo's hand darts out and grabs the bills meant for Pasquale.

THÉO

C'mon, drink. Drink up, it's on me.

Laughter.

Don't you want it? Fine, that's okay.

He empties the glass in one gulp, grimacing. Then he waves the bills while refilling Pasquale's glass.

THÉO

Panting.

This? You want this? If you do, you'll have to come outside and play your music for us.

Bottle in hand, Théo grabs Pasquale and, helped by Adrien and Isidore, drags him toward the door. Pasquale struggles to get away.

THÉO

C'mon, play!

PASQUALE

Let me go!

[Lasciatemi!]

Covered passage. Exterior. Night.

Outside, the fight continues. Pasquale manages to break free and run away, leaving behind his barrel organ.

THÉO

Shouting.

Hey, macaroni, play us some music! Don't go!

Isidore takes the instrument by the handles, shouting as he pushes it along. Théo jumps up on it, and Adrien starts to turn the crank. Shouting, drinking and laughing to the sound of the music, they disappear into the night.

Giuseppe's workroom. Interior. Night.

Sitting at his table, Giuseppe licks and seals an envelope. Carmelo is working in a corner of the room.

GIUSEPPE

Getting up.

There. Carmelo, take this to Pietro Fichera. He said he was going to St. Zénon tomorrow morning. Tell him that when he gets there, he should ask for Alphonse Lamoureux. Everyone there knows him.

[Ecco fatto! Carmelo, porta questo a Pietro Fichera. Domani mattina deve andare dalle parti de St. Zénon. Dicci che quando arriva 'o paisi deve dumandar per Alphonse Lamoureux, lo consocono tutti.]

CARMELO

Taking the letter.

You can trust me.

[Ci penso io.]

Carmelo disappears, then returns, carrying his coat over his arm.

GIUSEPPE

Where are you going? Take the alley, it's faster. It's late.

In a paternal tone, laying his hand on Carmelo's shoulder.

Carmelo, I'm counting on you. Tell Pietro to give it to him personally. Got that? Don't forget.

[Unni vai? Passa dalla ruelle che fai prima; è già tardi, chillo va a letto, dai. Carmelo, mi raccomando, eh? Digli che la lettera deve consegnargliela di persona. Capito? Non tu scurdari!]

CARMELO

Okay, okay.

[Sì, sì.]

He leaves.

GIUSEPPE

Shouting after him.

And come right back!

[E ritiriti presto!]

Giuseppe sits back down at the table, unfolds his newspaper and begins to read. All is quiet in the house, when Pasquale bursts in, obviously upset. He glances quickly inside the workroom, then begins to shout toward the stairway.

Joe! Melo! Carmelo! Where are you? Come down! They stole my organ!

[Joe! Melo! Carmelo...! Unni siti...? Scinniti! Mi pigghiarunu u pianino.]

Giuseppe gets up and walks over to him, worried.

GIUSEPPE

What's going on, Pasquale?

[Che è sta storia, Pasquale?]

PASQUALE

It's that guy from the church. He and his friends stole my organ.

[Chiddu da chiesa, co' gli amici suoi mi pigghiarunu u pianino.]

Pasquale walks quickly to his room. Joe and Melo come downstairs. They all follow Pasquale.

Pasquale and Carmelo's room.
Interior Night.

Pasquale lifts up a corner of his mattress and takes out his knife. Giuseppe, Joe and Melo look on from the doorway.

JOE

Pasquale, what is it?

[Pasquali che t'è successo?]

PASQUALE

Come with me to Lavoie's tavern! That son of a bitch took my organ!

[Venite con me a taverna de Lavoie...! Ddi son-of-a-birch mi pigghiarunu u pianino!]

GIUSEPPE

Holding him back.

Calm down, Pasquale.

[Calmati, Pasquà...]

PASQUALE

How can I calm down? They're drunk. They'll smash it to bits!

[Ma che mi calmo! Chiddi sù nbriachi fradici e me rompono u pianino.]

GIUSEPPE

What are you planning, a bloodbath? Where are they? At Lavoie's?

[Senti, cosa vogliamo fare? Un macello? Dove sono? Da Lavoie?]

PASQUALE

Yes.

[Sì.]

GIUSEPPE

I'll go and take care of everything.

[Ci vado subito io e sistemo tutto.]

PASQUALE

Shouting.

Peppe... they're like mad dogs. They don't give a shit about what you have to say.

[Peppe... chilli sono cani arraggiati e delle tue chiacchiere se ne fottono un cazzo.]

He breaks away.

GIUSEPPE

Stop it. Give me your knife.

[Unni vai! Leva stu cuteddu ti dissi!]

Pasquale stops and turns to Giuseppe.

PASQUALE

Peppe, mind your own business! I pay my rent, so I can do what I want.

[Peppe, fatti i cazzu tuoi, io ti pago il bordo, di conseguenza faccio quello che mi pare e piace.]

Giuseppe grabs him and throws him against the wall.

GIUSEPPE

Look, Pasquale, this is my house. Got that? If you don't like it, you can take your things and leave. I said I'd go and get your organ. You have my word.

[Senti, Pasquale, questa è casa mia, capisti? Se vuoi fare di testa tua, ti pigli le cose tue e te ne vai. T'ho detto che ci vado io e ti riporto il tuo pianino, parola mia.]

As he says this, Giuseppe offers his hand. Pasquale extends his, though reluctantly.

GIUSEPPE

To Joe and Melo.

You two stay with him.

[Voi pure, restate qui cu iddu.]

Giuseppe walks away.

Front hall of Moschella's house.
Interior. Night.

In the foreground, Ninetta is standing near the staircase. Giuseppe hurries down the hall, taking his coat from a hook as he goes by.

NINETTA

What's he done now?

[Ni cumminau n'autra chiddu?]

Without answering, Giuseppe heads toward the door. Off-camera we hear shouting and music from the barrel organ. Giuseppe stops, worried, then disappears into the workroom. Ninetta follows after him. In the backround, Melo appears in the kitchen doorway. The music comes closer and closer.

MELO

Pasquale, your organ!

[Pasquale, l'organetto!]

Melo runs out, followed by Joe and Pasquale. They all enter the workroom. Ninetta looks at them without understanding.

THÉO

Hey, macaroni, we brought your music box!

ISIDORE

And your money, too!

From the window of the workroom, we see Adrien and Isidore leaning against the barrel organ, and Théo, drinking from the bottle.

THÉO

C'mon! Come and get it.

ISIDORE

There he is, Théo. I can see him!

ADRIEN

He's scared stiff!

From the workroom window, Giuseppe, Pasquale and Melo watch on.

PASQUALE

I told you they're drunk!

[Tu dissi chi ssù mbriachi!]

Outside, Théo approaches and waves toward the window.

THÉO

Hey, beggar, you afraid? Come and get it!

Pasquale tries to go outside, but Melo holds him back.

PASQUALE

Let's go!

[Venite cu mmìa!]

GIUSEPPE

You stay here, goddammit! I said I'll handle this.

[Tu là resta, porco Dio! T'ho detto che ci penso io!]

ISIDORE

Hey, Pasquale! Look, Pasquale!

They all return to the window. Outside, Théo is pouring the contents of the bottle over the barrel organ, dousing his friends as he does.

THÉO

Turning toward the window.

If you don't come out, we'll set your little mouth organ on fire!

PASQUALE

Bandits!

[Disonesti!]

Raging, Pasquale lunges toward the door. Giuseppe, Melo and Joe race after him.

Front hall of Moschella's house.
Interior. Night.

Giuseppe catches Pasquale and holds him firmly by the arm. Pasquale has taken out his knife. Giuseppe tries to wrestle it from him. Joe and Melo arrive to help.

PASQUALE

Let go of me, you bastards! Let go of me!

[Lassatimi pugnu de bastardi! Lassatimi!]

JOE

Shouting.

Stop it! Stop it! Don't you see they're trying to provoke you? Are you going to fall for it?

[Fermo! Fermo! Non vedi che ceccùnu a provocazione! E tu come nu scemu ci voi iri!]

GIUSEPPE

Also shouting.

Drop it! Drop that knife!

[Lassalu...! Lassa stu cuteddu!]

After much effort, the three men manage to immobilize Pasquale, and Giuseppe can finally take away his knife. Panting, he folds the blade back into the handle and tosses it away.

GIUSEPPE

To Joe and Melo.

Hold him tight.

[Tenetelo fermo.]

He walks out.

Outside Moschella's house. Exterior. Night.

Théo continues to drink from the bottle, while Isidore tries to grab it away from him. Giuseppe appears at his doorstep. Isidore sees him and points with his finger.

ISIDORE

Théo, look!

Théo turns around.

THÉO

Who're you?

GIUSEPPE

What's your problem?

Théo laughs and turns toward his friends.

THÉO

Who is this guy?

He continues to douse the organ with the contents of the bottle, splattering Adrien, who manages to wrest the bottle from him. The two men laugh as they totter. Théo gestures toward Giuseppe.

THÉO

Who's he?

GIUSEPPE

Gravely.

Giuseppe Moschella.

THÉO

Laughing.

Ah, my father-in-law's tailor!

Adrien and Isidore laugh and shout derisively.

GIUSEPPE

Look, Alphonse is my friend, and you know it. And among friends, there are ways to talk.

THÉO

Becoming aggressive.

Where's the beggar hiding?

GIUSEPPE

Look, don't you think he's made enough trouble already? I told him to stay inside.

Théo overturns the organ. Laughter. He walks toward Giuseppe, belting out the wedding march from Lohengrin.

THÉO

Tam tam ta tam!

ADRIEN

Watch it, Théo. He'll cut you, too!

Théo puts his arm around Giuseppe, who tries to push him away, but gently, so as not to provoke a fight.

THÉO

With a syrupy voice.

A fine suit you made for his wedding.

Renewed laughter and mocking exclamations.

You told him to stay inside?

GIUSEPPE

Yes.

THÉO

So you're the one making trouble!

GIUSEPPE

No, I'm not. This is my home.

THÉO

Threatening.

Go get the beggar right now!

GIUSEPPE

If you don't stop, I'll get the police.

THÉO

Ah, he's going to get the police! Hear that, guys?

Laughter.

Bring him out!

Théo pushes Giuseppe away. Giuseppe is beginning to lose his temper.

GIUSEPPE

No, he stays put. Look, Alphonse and I are friends. Understand?

ISIDORE

Hey, macaroni! Go tell that bum to come for his music box.

ADRIEN

Shouting.

Hey, Pasquale, I'm going to give it a try. I bet I play good, huh, guys?

GIUSEPPE

Raising his voice, to Théo.

Take your pals and clear out!

THÉO

Shouting.

Listen, my pals are talking to you! Open your ears!

ADRIEN

This'll warm things up.

Giuseppe turns to Adrien.

GIUSEPPE

Shouting.

Hey, don't do that!

Giuseppe walks toward Adrien, who is holding a match above the whiskey-soaked organ.

GIUSEPPE

Calmer.

Stop that, leave us alone.

Laughter.

What do you want?

A brief moment of silence. No one moves. Finally, Giuseppe takes a few steps and stoops to right the organ. Straightaway, Théo jumps on him, throws him to the ground and kicks him in the stomach.

THÉO

Shouting.

Don't touch that! ...You, keep out of this! Now go get him and tell him we want to give this back to him in person. Go, go!

Théo kicks and prods Giuseppe toward the house. Adrien follows them, clapping his hands and cackling as if he were chasing a chicken.

ADRIEN

Faster, faster, faster!

Front hall of Moschella's house.
Interior. Night.

Ninetta rushes to meet Giuseppe.

NINETTA

Anxiously.

Did they hurt you?

[Che, ti fecero male?]

GIUSEPPE

Roughly pushing her away.

Leave me alone!

[Lasciami stare.]

NINETTA

Devastated.

Giuseppe, what are you doing?

[Giuseppe, che fai?]

From the kitchen, where Joe has led Pasquale, the two men watch Giuseppe go to a cupboard, open it frantically, and take out a revolver. Seeing this, Ninetta tries to block his way. Melo appears in the doorway to the workroom.

NINETTA

Shouting.

Have you lost your mind?

[Che niscisti pazzu?]

GIUSEPPE

Shut up! You'll see. They'll shit their pants.

[Muta tu! Vi fazzu videri io comu si cacunu i sotto.]

Ninetta grabs his arm, desperately trying to hold him back.

NINETTA

Where are you going?

[Unni vai?]

GIUSEPPE

Struggling.

Let go!

[Lassame!]

NINETTA

Screaming, not letting go.

Where are you going?

[Unni vai?]

Giuseppe shakes himself free. Joe and Pasquale rush over to the window. Panting and terrified, Ninetta remains alone at the half-open door and watches what happens outside. The camera slowly moves in on her as the drama unfolds on the other side of the door.

GIUSEPPE

Get away from that!

ISIDORE

Hey, take it easy!

GIUSEPPE

I'm telling you for the last time... Go away and leave us alone!

Yelling.

Move! Move away... *dai!*

ISIDORE

Okay, we're going.

THÉO

Hey, Mr. Tailor, that ain't no pair of scissors!

Laughter.

ISIDORE

His voice tense.

C'mon, Théo, let's go. Forget it, forget it.

THÉO

No, let go of me!

GIUSEPPE

Get off me!

THÉO

C'mon, hand it over!

GIUSEPPE

Get off!

THÉO

In a rage.

You bastard, I'll show you!

ISIDORE

Yelling.

Théo!

ADRIEN

Yelling.

Go on, Théo! Bust his face! Bust his fat wop face!

ISIDORE

Théo, no!

We hear two people fighting, then a gunshot. Ninetta shudders.

ISIDORE

Incredulous.

Théo?

Shouting.

Théo!

In the silence, we hear Giuseppe run off. Trembling, Ninetta closes the door, frozen with terror.

NINETTA

In a murmur.

We're ruined!

[N'arruvinasti!]

Country road. Exterior. Day.

A hearse crosses the empty countryside, carrying Théo's body.

Parlour at Alphonse's house in St. Zénon. Interior. Night.

Little Rita has fallen asleep in Margie's lap. We hear people saying the rosary. Alphonse goes over to the little girl, lifts her gently in his arms so as not to wake her, and heads for the staircase that leads upstairs.

A small group surrounds the body laid out in the casket. A kneeling woman recites Aves, to which those present reply. Opposite her are Félicité, Léon and Father Phaneuf.

The priest crosses himself and walks out of the room and toward the front door. Félicité whispers something into Léon's ear and also goes to the front hall.

Hallway at Alphonse's house.
Interior. Night.

FÉLICITÉ

Thank you for coming, Father.

The priest shakes his head with emotion.

FATHER PHANEUF

Poor Théo, I can't believe it...

Félicité reaches for the priest's coat and helps him into it.

FATHER PHANEUF

But you know, Félicité, every misfortune bears with it a seed of hope.

Félicité hands him his hat.

The good Lord, in his great wisdom, has brought you back to us. To St. Zénon, where you'll take your place again.

He places his hand on Félicité's arm.

I'm here to help you.

Félicité answers with a slight nod of her head. The priest leaves. Félicité closes the door.

FÉLICITÉ

Did she wake up?

ALPHONSE

Tenderly.

No, no, don't worry.

Félicité returns to the parlour. Someone knocks at the door. Alphonse opens, and Isidore steps in. Alphonse offers his hand.

ALPHONSE

Surprised.

Isidore? We didn't expect you until tomorrow, for the funeral.

ISIDORE

Taking off his coat.

I decided to come this evening. I managed to catch the last train.

Alphonse takes Isidore's coat.

ISIDORE

I have news. The Italian gave himself up to the police.

ALPHONSE

When?

ISIDORE

This morning.

Alphonse turns away to hang up the coat.

We'll get him, just you wait.

Alphonse is shaken by the news. With a weary gesture, he points toward the parlour.

ALPHONSE

In a broken voice.

Go ahead, everyone's inside.

Isidore disappears. Alphonse remains alone, sad and brooding.

Courthouse. Corridor outside the courtroom. Interior. Day.

Giuseppe is seated on a bench between two policemen. A third policeman arrives and motions them to stand up. The first policeman opens the door leading to the courtroom and steps aside to let Giuseppe through. The door closes.

Moschella's workroom. Interior. Day.

Ninetta dips her pen in the inkwell and slowly begins to write in her notebook. She is keeping a diary. Scenes from the trial are intercut with Ninetta's description of it.

We see the following scenes: Giuseppe in the dock, a guard on either side of him; Pasquale being questioned by the crown attorney; Félicité, sitting next to Adrien, as she slowly turns to stare at Ninetta; and Giuseppe, being questioned by the crown attorney and his own lawyer.

NINETTA

'First day of the trial. Giusé was as pale as death. He looked at me only once. The man who wants to have him found guilty had eleven people speak. The dead man's widow spoke too. I didn't understand all they said. Then they called me to the front, but I couldn't open my mouth. I have to go back tomorrow. What's the point of all this? Who can change destiny?'

['Primo iorno du procedsso. Giuseppe era pallido como a morti. Mi guardò na volta sola. Chiddu che vole fare condannare Giuseppe fece parlare undici persone. Anche la mugghieri du morto parlò. Non capii bonu che dissero. Poi mi fecero veniri avanti, ma non riuscii a aprire la bocca. Mi fanno tornare domani. A cosa servi tutto chistu? Chi può canciare o destino?']

All rise as the judge enters.

NINETTA

'Third day. They had seven people speak today. Monsieur Alphonse was alone. The widow has stopped coming. Giuseppe didn't look at me once.'

['Terzo iorno. Oggi hanno fatto parlare sette persone. Monsieur Alphonse era solo. La mugghieri du morto non venne più. Manco oggi Giuseppe mi guardau.']

In the courtroom, we see the prosecutor pointing the murder weapon at Giuseppe. We then see Giuseppe's lawyer address the jury and later the judge leave the courtroom.

NINETTA

'Fourth day. Giuseppe said that he's not a murderer. Everyone began to laugh. He repeated it twice. But then the judge told him to be quiet. A curse on him! Giuseppe's lawyer made a long speech. Everyone listened attentively. He must be good. Tomorrow the judge will speak. What will he say? Will I be able to hold on till then?'

['Quarto iorno. Giuseppe disse che lui non è un assassino. La gente si mise a ridere. Lui lo ripetio du vote. Ma poi u giudice non lo fece chiù parlari. Malanova a iddu. L'avvocato di Giuseppe fece un lungo discorso tutti o sentirono con attenzione. Deve essere bravo. Mi disse che domani parla il giudice. Cosa dirà? Riuscirò a resistere fino a domani.']

Front hall of Moschella's house.
Interior. Day.

Joe, Pasquale and Carmelo enter in silence, their heads bowed. They're wearing their finest clothes. Melo comes out to meet them.

MELO

Well? How did it go in court?

[Com'è finita in tribunale?]

JOE

Badly. We'll talk about it later. Where's the signora?

[Male, male... poi ne parliamo. La signora dov'è?]

MELO

She hasn't left her room all morning.

[È stat chiusa into la camera tutta la mattina.]

Joe looks toward the top of the staircase, hesitates, and turns to Pasquale.

JOE

Pasquale, you tell her.

[Pasquale 'inchiana tu a dircelo.]

PASQUALE

Me? What'll I say? You go.

[Io? E che ccià diri? Vacci tu.]

Melo grows impatient and takes Joe's arm.

MELO

Well?

[E allora?]

They all turn toward Carmelo, who has remained off to one side, leaning against the wall.

CARMELO

I'll tell her.

[Ci vado a dircelo.]

The three men look at him expectantly. Carmelo walks slowly up the stairs. Ninetta is waiting for him at the top, leaning against the railing. On seeing Carmelo's stricken face, she realizes that all is lost. She turns away and disappears into her room. With a gesture of helplessness, Carmelo goes back downstairs.

Moschella's workroom. Interior. Night.

The four boarders are in the workroom. Carmelo is seated at the table, laboriously reading aloud from La Patrie. *Behind him, Pasquale paces back and forth, drinking his coffee. Joe is seated at one end of the table, solemnly smoking a cigar.*

CARMELO

Turning to Pasquale.

They printed the judge's entire speech. Listen: 'The unfortunate situation in which you find yourself at present can only be ascribed to the custom adopted by you and many of your compatriots of keeping weapons at home or carrying them on you. This practice goes against the laws and customs of Canada...'

[Hanno scritto tutto quello che ha detto il giudice. Senti...]

Melo, who doesn't understand French, sits down beside Carmelo.

MELO

Impatiently.

Well? What's it say?

[Allora? Che dice?]

CARMELO

It says we're not allowed to keep guns at home.

[Stà scritto che non possiamo tenere pistole dentro a casa.]

Pasquale is indignant.

PASQUALE

Che son of a bitch!

CARMELO

'...and has previously involved foreigners like yourself in of-
fenses that led to long prison terms. It is our hope that this
sentence may serve as a warning to all who may be tempted
to use dangerous weapons.'

MELO

Impatiently.

Go on, translate!

[Dai, traduci, dai.]

CARMELO

It says they want to teach us a lesson, to make us stop doing
it.

[Dice che ci imparano una lezione, così non la facciamo
chiù sta cosa.]

PASQUALE

Don Peppe was too honest. But what do they know about
being honest?

[Lui ha voluto fare troppo l'onesto. Ma questi la capiscono
l'onestà?]

JOE

I always said don Peppe was wrong to give himself up.

Losing his temper.

If I was him, I would've run.

[L'ho sempre detto... Don Giuseppe ha fato male a consti-
tuirsi. Io al posto suo me ne fossi iusto.]

In the background, we see Ninetta coming down the stairs.

MELO

Getting up.

They want don Peppe to serve as a lesson.

[Hanno voluto dar l'esempio con don Peppe.]

*Seeing Ninetta, who greets them with a nod, he stops. The
others watch in silence as she pulls on a shawl and heads toward
the kitchen.*

PASQUALE

Well, I better go to work. See you.

[Picciotti, io me ne vado a travagghiare, vi saluto.]

JOE

Wait, Pasquale. I'll come, too.

[Aspetta Pasquàli, vengo pure io.]

*Pasquale and Joe leave. Melo slowly climbs the stairs to his
room. Carmelo remains alone in the workroom.*

Alberto Celi's reception room.
Interior. Night.

*A banner is strung between the columns of the hall:
Moschella vivo! Standing on the rostrum, Celi is declaiming the-
atrically. Seated behind him are Ninetta, Salvatore in uniform,*

lawyer Saint-Louis, and a priest, father Leonardo. The audience consists of some thirty listeners, including a few notables, along with Joe, Melo, Pasquale and Angelo Lopinto.

CELI

Emphatically.

I, Alberto Celi, an Italian, ask all my friends, in the name of poor Giuseppe Moschella — who was sentenced to death for committing a murder in self-defence — to make a heartfelt offering in order to raise the sum needed to pay the costs of the worthy lawyer who will defend him in the Court of Appeals. This terrible sentence must be commuted! We want Moschella to live! All generous Italians can send their donations to 1206 Notre Dame Street East, Montreal.

Celi pauses briefly before continuing in Italian.

I paid for this article out of my own pocket to be the first to set an example. This isn't simply a question of saving our poor Moschella, but also of protecting the honour of us all, Italians of Montreal.

Sweeping with his arm toward Salvatore.

We have with us tonight Comandante Moschella, who has just arrived from Italy!

[Questo articolo l'ho pagato di tasca mia per essere il primo a dare l'esempio. Non si tratta solo di salvare il nostro povero Moschella ma anche di proteggere l'onore di noi tutti, Italiani de Montreal. E poi c'è qui con noi il comandante Moschella appena arrivato dall'Italia!]

Celi invites him to stand. Salvatore does so. Applause.

CELI

Dear friends, this country should be grateful to us Italians. Who was the first to discover the Americas?

[Cari amici, questo paese deve essere riconoscente verso gli Italiani. Chi è stato il primo a scoprire le Americhe?]

SPECTATOR

Columbus! An Italian!

[Colombo! Un italiano!]

In the back of the hall, off to one side, Pasquale is listening to Celi. Angelo Lopinto walks over to Pasquale, his violin under his arm, and stops to whisper a few words in his ear. Then, with a nod of his head, he invites Pasquale to follow him. Pasquale hesitates for a second, then gets up.

ANGELO

That guy's not getting my money.

[Io a quello i miei soldi non glieli do.]

PASQUALE

Mine either.

[Mano io.]

Angelo takes a banknote from his pocket and hands it to Pasquale.

ANGELO

Here. Give this to signora Moschella. I'll tell Pietro and Bastiano to do the same. You know, the musicians in Ville Émard.

[To... daglieli tu alla signora Moschella. Ci dico di fare la stessa cosa a Pietro e a Bastiano... sai quelli che giocano a Ville Émard.]

PASQUALE

Taking the money.

All right...

[Sì, sì...]

ANGELO

I have to get to work. See you. Bye, Pasquale.

[Mo me ne devo andà a lavorà. Ci vediamo. Ciao, Pasquà.]

PASQUALE

See you!

[Saluti!]

Pasquale takes his place again. On the rostrum, Celi ends his speech with grandiloquence.

CELI

...a country that brought civilization to the entire world, including here to Montreal!

[...è un paese che ha insegnato la civiltà ovunque e anche qui a Montreal!]

Warm applause.

Parlour in Alphonse's house in
St. Zénon. Interior. Day.

Félicité enters the parlour, picks up a newspaper from a desk and glances at the headlines. She notices an envelope addressed to Ninetta. Opening it, she finds a letter and some money.

Outside Alphonse's house in
St. Zénon. Exterior. Day.

Félicité is pacing on the veranda, deeply upset. We hear a carriage pull up and stop. Félicité pauses at the top of the stairs, staring at Alphonse, who is off-screen, but whom we then see step down from his carriage and walk briskly toward the house.

ALPHONSE

Climbing the stairs.

I forgot something.

Félicité pulls the letter and money from her pocket.

FÉLICITÉ

Is this what you forgot?

With an abrupt gesture, she throws them in his face. Alphonse stands there, speechless. Félicité walks to the door, then turns to her father.

FÉLICITÉ

You have to be pretty generous to give money to murderers!

She slams the door. Alphonse is dumbstruck.

Prison visiting room. Interior. Day.

Behind a metal grill, Giuseppe's stricken face. He finally breaks the silence.

GIUSEPPE

Do you remember, at Messina? Two days waiting for the boat.

[Ti ricordi a Messina? Aspettammo la nave per due giorni.]

On the other side of the grill, Ninetta and Salvatore.

SALVATORE

With a paternal smile.

We never wanted you to leave.

[E no che non volevamo che tu partissi.]

Short silence.

GIUSEPPE

How are your kids?

[Comu su i picciriddi?]

SALVATORE

They've grown!

[Eh! sono cresciuti!]

GIUSEPPE

They must be big by now, huh?

[Ora ann'à essere grandi? eh!]

SALVATORE

You should see them!

[Eh... Dovresti vederli!]

Another silence, which Giuseppe breaks.

GIUSEPPE

What do people say at home?

[Cosa dice la gente al paese?]

SALVATORE

Back home? What should they say? You're not the first, and you won't be the last. You remember Turi Nicotra in Philadelphia? That's America. But you wouldn't listen.

[A gente? E che deve dire a gente? Non sei il primo né sarai l'ultimo. Ti ricordi di Turi Nicotra a Filadelfia? Chista è l'America... ! Ma tu non l'hai mai voluto capire.]

GIUSEPPE

I'm not a gangster like Turi! I always respected the law. I've always been an honest citizen. But now people think I'm a murderer, a dirty criminal!

[Io non sono Turi u malandrino! Io la legge l'ho sempre rispettata. Mi sono comportato sempre come un galantuomo. Ma ormai per la gente sono un assassino, uno sporco criminale.]

NINETTA

Giuseppe, do you realize everything that people are doing for you?

[Giuseppe u sai che sta facendo la gente per tia?]

SALVATORE

That's right. And justice has yet to take its course.

[Sì, certo, e poi la giustizia non ha ancora finito il suo corso.]

GIUSEPPE

You call this justice?

Shouting.

Those bums should be in here, not me! They might've killed me. I mean, I did everything to avert a bloodbath, and they send me to the gallows!

[Me la chiami giustizia questa! Iddi dovrebbero stare qua dentro, non io. Quelli mi potevano anche ammazzare. Fino alla fine ho fatto di tutto per evitare na guerra e questi ti mandano diritto alla forca!]

SALVATORE

Giuseppe... !

GIUSEPPE

I'm not crazy. Sure, I know I fired. And that poor bastard paid with his life. But I'm no example! An example of what?

[...Non sono pazzo... E vero, il colpo è partito e quel disgraziato ci ha rimesso la pelle... Ma io non sono un esempio! Che è questo esempio!]

SALVATORE

Giusé... Calm down. Calm down.

[Giusé... Calmati... Calmati...]

GIUSEPPE

Lowering his voice.

A murderer. A murderer. People here respected me, and not only Italians.

[Assassino, assassino. La gente qui mi teneva nella palma di una mano, e non solo gli Italiani.]

Unable to hold back his tears, Giuseppe hides his face in his hands. Touched and embarrassed, Salvatore motions to Ninetta to leave them alone. Ninetta doesn't respond.

SALVATORE

In a low but authoritarian voice.

Go on!

[Vai!]

Ninetta gets up reluctantly. Sad and resigned, she sits down on a bench a few yards away. She finds the wait long. When Salvatore finally comes over, she quickly gets to her feet.

SALVATORE

Go on. Giuseppe wants to talk to you.

[Vai! Giuseppe tu vuole parlare.]

Ninetta goes to Giuseppe, her face anxious.

GIUSEPPE

Listen... I had my brother come over to take you home.

[Senti, a mi frate u fici veniri cusi ti porta o paise.]

NINETTA

Stunned.

Where, home?

[Quale paisi?]

GIUSEPPE

Ninetta. I don't want you to stay here alone.

[Ninetta. Non voglio che tu resti cca sola.]

Ninetta shakes her head.

NINETTA

But I want to be near you.

[Io cca resto vicino a tia.]

Giuseppe grows impatient.

GIUSEPPE

I told you that you should go. America's no place for a woman alone.

[Ti dissi che tu ne devi andare... L'America non è ppè fimmini suli!]

Ninetta flares up in turn.

NINETTA

You can say what you like. But neither God nor Satan can make me leave. Understand?

[Ti stai facennu i cunti di testa tua! A me di qua non mi smuove ne Salvatore ne u Patri eternu..., u capisti?]

Ninetta shouts in the direction of Salvatore, who is standing a few steps behind.

NINETTA

And you, understand?

[Magari tu, u capisti?]

Getting no response, she stands up, goes over to him and tugs his arm.

NINETTA

Do you understand?

[U capisti?]

Salvatore doesn't know how to respond. To avoid a scene and to shut her up, he pretends to acquiesce.

SALVATORE

All right. We'll discuss this at home. Now say goodbye.

With contained rage.

Go on!

[D'accordo. Ne parliamo a casa, va bene? Adesso, saluta tuo marito e andiamo. Dai!]

Ninetta returns to the bench and her belongings.

NINETTA

To Giuseppe.

I brought your sweater, as you asked.

[Ti purtai a maglia comu mi dicisti tu...]

She leaves without saying goodbye, Salvatore following her. The guard closes the heavy iron door.

Moschella kitchen. Interior. Night.

Salvatore is alone at the kitchen table, eating slowly, enjoying his dinner. Carmelo appears in the corridor; he takes a few steps, then goes into the kitchen to see if the captain has finished his meal. Sensing someone behind him, the captain turns around. Their eyes meet. Indifferent, Salvatore goes on with his meal, and Carmelo turns to leave.

Melo's room at Moschella's house.
Interior. Night.

Joe has been moved in with Melo to make room for the captain. The two Ingrassia brothers are seated on their bed, playing cards. Carmelo enters.

JOE

So, Carmelo, is the comandante finished yet?

[Allora Carmelo sto comandante ha finito?]

CARMELO

He eats like a gentleman... no rush.

[Quello come un signore mangia... no rush.]

MELO

Irritated.

He gets his own room while we're packed in like sardines.

[E ci ha la stanza tutta per lui... e noi siamo qui come le sardine...]

JOE

Does Pasquale have friends in Toronto?

[Pasquale tiene qualcuno a Toronto?]

MELO

I don't know.

[Bo!]

CARMELO

What's the guy up to?

[Chi lo capise sto cristiano.]

JOE

Aggravated.

He wants us to stay in here so he can talk to the signora alone.

[Ma vuole che restiamo qui perché deve parlare con la signora da solo.]

MELO

So he can touch her ass.

[Gli deve toccare u culu...]

JOE

Keep quiet!

[Ei zitto nu poco.]

Joe gives his cousin a slap on the head.

MELO

Hey! Keep your paws to yourself.

[Ei! Sempre con le mani ci stai tu.]

JOE

Then play!

[Sì, ma gioca!]

MELO

I did!

[Ho giocato!]

Moschella kitchen. Interior. Night.

Pasquale enters and goes over to Ninetta, who is tasting the soup. She curtly invites him to sit down at the table.

NINETTA

Sit down, supper's ready.

[Assettate, che un altro poco si mangia.]

PASQUALE

Sorry, I can't, signora. I'll miss my train.

[Nun posso signora, prendo il treno, grazie.]

Ninetta crosses her arms and stands in front of Pasquale.

NINETTA

What do you mean?

[Che è sta novità?]

PASQUALE

I'm going to Toronto. I sent my organ on ahead. I've been here in Montreal too long. Signora... take this money.

[Parto per Toronto. U piano lo spedia stamani. E troppo tempo che sono cca a Montreal. Signora, si pigliasse sti soldi.]

He hands her a wad of bills.

NINETTA

For what?

[Picchi?]

PASQUALE

From us musicians... for your husband.

Ninetta turns away.

Signora Antonietta, take it, I beg you.

[Mi desuru i miei compagni suonatori, è per la causa di suo marito. Signora Antonietta, se li pighiasse per carità.]

Ninetta takes the money, holding Pasquale's hand in hers.

NINETTA

Thanks, Pasquale.

[Grazie, Pasquale.]

Pasquale leaves the kitchen, then returns, carrying his suit-case. He passes in front of Salvatore.

PASQUALE

Goodbye, Comandante.

[Lo saluto comandante.]

He crosses the kitchen. Ninetta hastily removes her apron and follows him to the front door. Salvatore looks on, smoking. Ninetta helps Pasquale pull on his jacket.

PASQUALE

Thanks, signora.

[Grazie, signora.]

NINETTA

Goodbye, Pasquale.

[Addio, Pasquale.]

PASQUALE

Say hello to Peppe for me, and good luck.

Shouting upstairs.

Guys, I'm leaving. If you're ever in Toronto, look me up.

[Mi salutasse Peppe e tanti auguri. Picciotti, io parto, eh! Se passate per Toronto faceteme na visita, eh!]

CARMELO

Bye, Pasquale, see you!

[Ciao, Pasquà! Ci rivediamo eh!]

Pasquale disappears, closing the door behind him. Ninetta stands there, pensive, the money still in her hand. She slips it into her skirt pocket. Salvatore comes over.

SALVATORE

I didn't expect that from him.

Holding his hand out to Ninetta.

Where's the money?

[Questa proprio non me l'aspettavo da quel tipo lì... Dove sono i soldi?]

NINETTA

Without looking at him, indicating her pocket.

Here.

[Cca su...]

SALVATORE

Still holding out his hand.

Well, let me see it.

[Dai, fammeli vedere.]

NINETTA

Why? Didn't you see it?

[Pecché, ne vedisti prima?]

SALVATORE

Ninetta, it's best I keep it for you.

[Ninetta, è meglio che li tengo io.]

NINETTA

He gave it to me, and I'm keeping it.

[A mia mi desi, e io i tegnu.]

SALVATORE

Angry.

Give me the money!

[Tu, dammi sti soldi.]

Ninetta turns on her heels and hurries toward the stairs. Salvatore tries to grab her arm, but she pulls away and runs. Salvatore remains at the bottom of the stairs.

SALVATORE

Shouting, furious.

Come back here!

[Ei! torna qui!]

From upstairs we hear Ninetta's footsteps, and the door of her room slamming.

Attorney Thompson's office. Interior. Day.

Panelled walls, expensive furniture, paintings and objets d'art: the law office of Mr. Thompson. Ninetta, who sits very straight and still on her chair, holding her purse on her knees, is impressed. The white-haired lawyer is the very picture of respectability. From behind his desk, he listens attentively to the explanations offered by Giuseppe's lawyer. Ninetta, who can't speak English, carefully watches Thompson's face.

SAINT-LOUIS

In English.

I don't know how strong a case we can make on the self-defense issue. The premeditation argument, I think, is the weakest one... Moschella didn't even know the victim. And then there is the question of the jury; in their verdict there is a request for commutation, but they didn't make it explicit and the judge ignored it.

THOMPSON

In English.

Let me see the jury's item.

Saint-Louis hands him the document, and smiles encouragingly at Ninetta.

THOMPSON

In English.

I think there is a better chance with a straight request for clemency rather than going through the whole appeal procedure.

SAINT-LOUIS

Translating for Ninetta.

Mr. Thompson thinks we have a chance. In a few days, we'll go to the Ministry of Justice in Ottawa to present your husband's case. You mustn't give up hope, madame Moschella.

Ninetta opens her purse and pulls out a wad of bills which she proudly offers to Thompson. But her smile freezes on her lips:

she senses she has made a faux-pas. She turns toward Saint-Louis, who discreetly shakes his head 'No'.

NINETTA

To Thompson.

There's $200... Is that enough to save Giuseppe?

Saint-Louis gently pushes the money away and turns to Thompson with an indulgent smile.

SAINT-LOUIS

In English.

She asks if two hundred is enough...

THOMPSON

In English.

Tell her we'll worry about it later.

SAINT-LOUIS

Translating for Ninetta.

Don't worry, we'll see about that later.

Confused, Ninetta places the money in front of Thompson anyway. He pushes it away with a friendly smile.

THOMPSON

In English.

Later... Later...

Saint-Louis takes the money and gives it back to Ninetta.

THOMPSON

In English.

Cheer up, madame Moschella. I will do my best.

He stands up to end the meeting.

Tomorrow, ten o'clock sharp, Saint-Louis.

SAINT-LOUIS

In English.

All right.

Saint-Louis collects his papers. Thompson holds out his hand.

SAINT-LOUIS

In English.

Thank you, sir.

Stairway in the building of Thompson's office. Interior. Day.

Celi is climbing the stairs, in a rush. He stops for a second to get his bearings, then turns left down a corridor.

Thompson's office. Interior. Day.

The door to the office opens: Thompson's secretary lets Celi in. Seeing Saint-Louis and Ninetta, Celi is shocked.

CELI

Monsieur Saint-Louis, what's going on? Are you already finished?

Saint-Louis tries to draw him outside.

SAINT-LOUIS

Conciliatory.

No, everything's fine, monsieur Celi. Mr. Thompson has agreed to take on the case.

Put out, Celi turns to Ninetta.

CELI

Indignant.

Signora, why didn't you wait for me? Do you realize how you'll make me look to the committee?

[Ma, signora, perché non mi ha aspettato? Si rende conto che figura mi fa fare di fronte al nostro comitado?]

Without answering, Ninetta leaves the room. Celi turns to Saint-Louis.

CELI

Do you realize, attorney? I do everything to help that poor woman. But she takes things into her own hands.

SAINT-LOUIS

Please, Celi, calm down. Let's leave, we're disturbing Mr. Thompson.

They leave. The door closes. For a few seconds we continue to hear Celi's protests.

CELI

But I ask you, how can anyone act so irresponsibly, signora?

[Ma io mi domando e dico: come si può agire in maniera così irresponsabile, signora?]

Moschella's workroom. Interior. Night.

Her head propped on her fist, Ninetta writes in her notebook.

NINETTA

'Day of sorrow! The lawyers came back from Ottawa. The English lawyer says that only the Governor General of Canada can prevent his hanging. But Salvatore thinks the Governor General has other fish to fry. Who is this man? Celi says he'll write to the king of Italy and the Pope.'

['Che giornata disgraziata! Gli avvocati tornarono da Ottawa. L'avvocato inglese disse che solo il Governatore del Canada può impedire la morte. Ma Salvatore crede che sto' governatore avi altre cose da pensare. Chi è quest'uomo? Celi disse che scrive al Re d'Italia e al Papa.']

Country road. Exterior. Day.

A horse-cart travels across the sun-washed countryside, carrying Pietro Fichera, the carter, Ninetta, seated next to him, and Carmelo, in the back.

NINETTA

'He's nothing but a big talker. I'm afraid Giuseppe's days are numbered.'

['Chiddu le pensa tutte per fare i bei discorsi. Ma ormai Giuseppe ha i giorni contati.']

The cart is traversing the same countryside as the hearse that carried Théo's body in an earlier scene.

St. Zénon cemetery. Exterior. Day.

In a small cemetery, Carmela walks between the tombstones, reading the inscriptions. He finally finds Théo's grave and shouts to Ninetta, who has stayed with Pietro at the entrance to the cemetary.

CARMELO

Here it is, signora! I found it! Look.

[Sta ccà signora! A truvai. Iddu è.]

Ninetta rushes over to read the inscription and kneels before the grave. She crosses herself, then crouches on her heels. Carmelo also crosses himself. Ninetta turns halfway round to him and gestures, and he walks off, leaving her alone. Ninetta glances around, then opens the bag next to her on the ground. She takes out two slices of bread, which she places on the grave, and a bottle of wine. Clasping her hands, she murmurs an incantation.

NINETTA

Spirit who hears,

Spirit who sees,

Seek not Giuseppe's death.

Spirit who hears,

Spirit who sees,

Vent your rage on me.

Prickly thorns,

Lashing flames,

Flowing water,

and cries of men...

[Mortu chi senti,/Mortu chi vidi,/A morti i Giuseppe/Nun la circari. Mortu chi senti,/Mortu chi vidi,/A raggia tua a mia l'ha dari:/Spini pungenti/Focu ardenti/Acqua currenti/E gridi di genti...]

Ninetta takes the bottle and pours wine on the bread in the sign of a cross, then clasps her hands again.

Hail Mary, full of grace, the Lord is with Thee...

[Ave Maria, piena di grazia, il signore sia con te...]

Outside the presbytery. Exterior. Day.

Standing near the carter, who is smoking calmly, Carmelo looks around and sees Félicité walking toward the presbytery. He quickly turns away and lowers his head so he's not recognized.

CARMELO

To Pietro, under his breath.

The dead man's widow! Madonna, this'll turn out badly.

[A mugghieri du mortu! Madonna, cca e cose si mettunu male!]

Félicité arrives at the stairway leading to the presbytery. She turns to observe the carriage and the two men standing by the horse.

Recognizing Ninetta from afar, she strides over to her. Lost in prayer, Ninetta doesn't notice Félicité.

FÉLICITÉ

Shouting.

What are you doing?

Ninetta turns around, frightened.

What are you doing? What's all this garbage? Go back where you came from! Go back home, you damn Italian!

Ninetta sits, frozen to the spot. Carmelo runs over and pulls her away.

Still screaming.

And take your sorcery with you!

She kicks the wine and bread, then screams at Ninetta and Carmelo, who are running away.

FÉLICITÉ

Wasn't killing Théo enough? Go home, you goddamn foreigners!

Pietro, Ninetta and Carmelo climb hastily into the cart, which takes off down the road.

Office off Celi's reception hall.
Interior. Day.

Celi is dictating a telegram to Otello, his secretary, punctuating the text with eloquent gestures.

CELI

The entire Italian colony implores you to intercede STOP.

[Nostra colonia intera supplica sua intercessionne STOP.]

The telephone rings. Otello lifts the receiver and hands it to Celo.

CELI

Hello, Mr. Attorney, sir! How are you? ...Incredible, Mr. Attorney! ...That's wonderful! ...That's wonderful, Mr. Attorney! ...Fine ...fine. Goodbye.

He hangs up, turns to Otello with emotion, takes him by the shoulders and shakes him vigorously.

Otello! We've saved him! ...They just announced his sentence has been commuted! ...The Governor gave in! ...I did it, Otello. I did it!

[Otello! Lo abbiamo salvato! Era l'annuncio della grazia! Il governatore ha ceduto! Ce l'ho fatta Otello! Ce l'ho fatta!]

Prison visiting room. Interior. Day.

Ninetta and Salvatore sit opposite Giuseppe on the other side of the grill. We first see the faces of Salvatore and Ninetta, then Giuseppe, who is looking emotionally at Ninetta. Salvatore gets up.

SALVATORE

I'll leave you two.

[Bene. Vi lascio soli...]

He walks away. Man and wife look at each other tenderly.

GIUSEPPE

If only they'd let you in... I want to touch you.

[Picchi non ti fannu trasere cca intra. Ti vurria tuccari.]

NINETTA

Smiling softly.

Me too.

Short silence.

At least the nightmare's over.

[Pure io. Almeno... stu brutto sogno è finito.]

GIUSEPPE

For you.

[Finito pi tia.]

NINETTA

Passionately.

But I'm here, two steps from you.

[Ma iù cca sugnu, a du passi di tia.]

Giuseppe looks tenderly at Ninetta, but then his mood changes: his face darkens, and he lowers his head.

GIUSEPPE

Softly.

Ninetta, I want you to return home.

[Ninetta, u stissu vogghio chi ti nni vai o paisi...]

Ninetta knits her brows, then continues calmly.

NINETTA

Don't talk about that. You should be happy they're not going to hang you.

[Non mi cuntari sta cosa. Devi esseri contentu chi non ti ficiu moriri.]

GIUSEPPE

Think for once! Do you think I can spend the rest of my life in here? Without going crazy?

[Ma che pensi tu? Pensi chi iù pozzu passari tutta à me vita cca intra? Senza nesciri pazzu?]

Ninetta smiles, full of hope.

NINETTA

But anything can happen.

[Ma e cose canciano nella vita.]

GIUSEPPE

I wish I had your imagination.

[Beata te che campi di fantasia.]

Ninetta remains silent, a helpless expression on her face. The waiting room door opens and Celi enters. Looking around, he sees Ninetta first, sitting opposite Giuseppe, then Salvatore. He heads toward him. Salvatore gets up, and the two men shake hands.

CELI

In a low voice.

Comandante... It's marvellous, Comandante! It's marvellous!

[Comandante... Che meraviglia, comandante! Che meraviglia!]

Salvatore's reserve contrasts with Celi's enthusiasm.

SALVATORE

Yes, it's almost a miracle.

[Certo, certo, è quasi un miracolo!]

CELI

We are the miracle, Comandante!

[Siamo noi, il miracolo, comandante!]

Celi turns to Giuseppe and Ninetta and waves to them with his hand. Then, taking Salvatore's arm, he leads him away. The men pace up and down the room.

But it's not over yet! We'll organize a big celebration in honour of your brother! A ball! Everyone will come, you'll see. We'll put on a real show. We deserve it.

[Ma le cose non finiscono qui! Faremo una grande festa in onore di suo fratello. Un ballo! Ci saranno tutti, vedrà, vedrà che festa, che spettacolo, ce lo meritiamo!]

Salvatore looks troubled.

Alphonse's home at St. Zénon.
Exterior. Day.

The countryside is bathed in sunshine, and still green, despite it being late fall. Alphonse appears with Léon and one of his friends. From off-screen we hear Carmelo's voice.

CARMELO

Monsieur Alphonse!

Recognizing Carmelo, Alphonse sends the boys ahead.

ALPHONSE

To the boys.

You go on.

When he reaches Alphonse, Carmelo removes his hat.

CARMELO

Madame Ninetta sent me to tell you she's going back to Italy with don Peppe's brother. This is for you.

Carmelo gives Alphonse a package.

ALPHONSE

What is it?

CARMELO

A *pignolata*. Do you remember? She made it for you once. The cake you ate at the house.

ALPHONSE

Thank you. When is she leaving?

CARMELO

In ten days. She told me to give you this, too.

He digs into his pocket and takes out an envelope, which he hands to Alphonse.

It's your money.

ALPHONSE

But why?

CARMELO

The money from Pasquale and the Italian musicians was enough for the lawyers. She doesn't need it anymore, so she's giving it back to you.

Alphonse tries to give him back the envelope.

ALPHONSE

No, give it to her, it may come in handy.

CARMELO

No, no...

Alphonse slips the envelope in his pocket.

ALPHONSE

In ten days, you say?

CARMELO

Yes, she's very unhappy. She doesn't want to go, but don Peppe wants her to leave. She thanks you for everything you've done.

Shaking Alphonse's hand.

Goodbye, monsieur Alphonse. I have to get back to Montreal.

ALPHONSE

Stay a while!

CARMELO

No, no.

ALPHONSE

Carmelo, wait a minute!

CARMELO

No, I have to go.

Carmelo walks off. Alphonse stands there a moment, then, with a warm smile, opens the package and breaks off a piece of cake, which he eats as he walks to the house.

Corridor at Moschella's house.
Interior. Day.

Ninetta closes the door to Salvatore's room, crumpling the train tickets in her hand. She then goes to her room and closes the door behind her. Salvatore, who is coming up the stairs, is puzzled. He goes to his room to find out what she's been doing.

Prison warden's office. Interior. Day.

Alphonse is waiting for the warden to arrive. Behind him, the office door is ajar. Langelier comes in, carrying a file, and closes the door. He walks toward his desk. Alphonse gets up.

LANGELIER

What can I do for you, monsieur...?

ALPHONSE

Lamoureux! Alphonse...

Alphonse sits down again. Langelier sits facing him, glancing one last time at his file, then looks at Alphonse inquisitively.

ALPHONSE

What I'm about to ask may sound strange.

Brief pause. Langelier motions to him to continue.

About the Italian prisoner, Moschella... His wife is leaving in a few days, she's going back to her country. I'd like you to let them see each other one last time, alone.

LANGELIER

Coldly.

This isn't the Salvation Army here, monsieur Lamoureux.

ALPHONSE

I know that, but it wouldn't be the first time that women visit prisoners here... in private.

LANGELIER

Sternly.

Exactly! Do you know what happened to my predecessor? No... Besides, I don't think Moschella deserves such treatment.

ALPHONSE

All I'm asking is a humanitarian gesture, not only for Moschella, but also his wife.

LAVOIE

You've picked the wrong man, monsieur Lamoureux.

He gets up, walks over to Lamoureux.

He was supposed to hang, he's alive. Isn't that enough? Believe me, we treat our criminals well here.

Alphonse also gets up.

ALPHONSE

Sir, Moschella was my tailor, and whatever you may think, I believe he was a victim of unfortunate circumstances, as was Théo Lemieux, my son-in-law.

He takes a few steps toward the door.

LANGELIER

Stunned.

You mean that Lemieux was... your daughter's husband?

Alphonse turns slowly and nods 'yes'.

ALPHONSE

Goodbye, sir.

He leaves. Langelier looks pensive.

A prison cell. Interior. Night.

The door opens: a guard lets in Ninetta, wrapped in a shawl and cloak. She is frightened.

GUARD

This way, madame.

She enters the room, furnished only with a table and two chairs. The guard closes the door behind her.

A little later, Ninetta is sitting at the table. The door hinges creak. Startled, Ninetta jumps to her feet: Giuseppe has just come in.

GIUSEPPE

What are you doing here? How come they let you in?

[Che fai ccà... picchi ti ficiru veniri?]

NINETTA

Shrugging her shoulders.

A guard came to get me at home. Maybe because I'm leaving.

[A guardia mi vinni a pigghiare à casa... Sarà picchi aia a partiri.]

Giuseppe looks behind him. The door closes. The couple look at each other in silence for a few moments. Giuseppe is wearing his prisoner's uniform. He takes a few steps toward Ninetta, then stops.

NINETTA

In a murmur.

Giuseppe!

She rushes to take him in her arms, kisses his face and neck.

NINETTA

Hold me tight, Giusé!

[Strincimi forti! Giusé!]

Giuseppe hasn't moved. Now, he gently frees himself from her embrace.

NINETTA

Sadly.

Giuseppe, it's me, your Ninetta.

[Giuseppe sono io, a to Ninetta...]

She lays her head on Giuseppe's shoulder. Ellipse.

A few minutes later, Ninetta and Giuseppe are sitting face to face. Ninetta strokes Giuseppe's hands.

GIUSEPPE

Have the boarders left?

[I bordanti sinni ieru già?]

NINETTA

No, they'll stay with Carmelo till the end of the month.

[No restunu cu Carmelo finu a fini du misi.]

GIUSEPPE

Have you sold the furniture?

[E i moboli i vinnisti già tutti?]

NINETTA

Carmelo's looking after that. He said he'll send the money to me back home.

[Ci pensa Carmelo... dissi chi poi mi manna i soddi o paisi.]

Giuseppe kisses her hands.

GIUSEPPE

I want you so.

[Quanto ti desiderai...]

Giuseppe lifts Ninetta's skirt, then kneels before her and kisses her thighs. Ninetta takes his head in her hands. Ellipse.

Ninetta is sitting at the table, toying with her wedding ring. Giuseppe is standing behind her.

GIUSEPPE

Did you take the tickets?

[Ti pigliasti i biglietti?]

Ninetta turns around, surprised, but doesn't answer.

GIUSEPPE

Do you think my brother's an idiot? Do you realize how you're behaving? Everyone's waiting for you back home. Uncle Saverio has done everything to help you. He's taking you on at his store, a few steps from your mother's home.

Flaring up.

What the hell do you want?

[Ma che pensi che mi frate è un picciriddu? Ti rendi conto di come ti stai comportando? Al paese tutti ti aspettano; zio Saverio ha fatto tanto per aiutarci. Ti fa travagghiare nel suo magazzino, è a due passi da tua madre... Ma che cazzo stai cercando?]

A beat. Giuseppe goes over to Ninetta, and puts his hands on her shoulders.

GIUSEPPE

Nina!

NINETTA

Shaking her head, imploring.

Don't make me leave, Giuseppe!

[Non mi fare partire Giuseppe!]

GIUSEPPE

Tenderly.

Ninetta!

Ninetta stands up abruptly and moves away.

GIUSEPPE

With controlled anger.

You're so stubborn! How many times have I told you there's nothing more for you here!

[Ci hai proprio a testa dura... Quante vote ti l'aiu a diri che ormai tu quà non hai più niente da fari!]

NINETTA

Sad, but firm.

No! My place is here, near you!

[No! u me postu è cca vicinu à tia!]

Seizing Ninetta by the shoulders, Giuseppe shakes her, as if this could make her come to her senses.

GIUSEPPE

Here, where? Where? In prison?

[Unni cca? unni cca? Cca intra?]

NINETTA

Barely audible.

Yes!

[Sì!]

GIUSEPPE

As if to himself.

My brother's right, everything in this country's upside-down!

[Ci ha ragione me frati, cca le cose sono proprio alla rovescia!]

NINETTA

Violently, her eyes gleaming with anger.

Leave your brother out of it!

[Lassa fora to frati!]

For a moment Giuseppe can't find words, then he continues, gently.

GIUSEPPE

Nina, I can never be at peace, knowing you're here alone.

[Nina, io non posso stare tranquillo sapendo che tu sei la fuori sola...]

NINETTA

Raising her voice, outraged.

Why? Are you afraid I'll end up a whore?

[Ma picchi tu pensi che vaiu a fare la puttana?]

GIUSEPPE

Raising his voice in turn.

Don't raise your voice! No one said anything about whores. It's not that — I have to look after my affairs.

[Vedi di non alzare la voce! Non si tratta di puttane, questo non è lo discurso, io ho da guardare gli affari miei!]

NINETTA

Shouting.

Your affairs? *Our* affairs! Ours!

[Ma quali affari tuoi? Gli affari nostri! Nostri!]

GIUSEPPE

Nina, I'm still your husband, aren't I? Holy Mary, Mother of God!

[Nina, vedi che sono tuo marito io eh? Mannaia o mundo ladro, mannaia!]

Softening, Giuseppe goes over to Ninetta to try to reason with her.

GIUSEPPE

Nina, this country isn't for you.

Taking her hands.

My love, this country is not our blood. So, Nina, if you're really my wife, please... I implore you, have the goodness to leave.

[Nina, sto paese non è per tia. Gioia mia, sta terra non è pane per i nostri denti. Allora Nina, se sei mia mugghieri, per carità, famme solo sta grazia tenn'a ghiri.]

Ninetta frees herself from him brusquely. Giuseppe takes Nina's cloak, which she had left on the table, and holds it out to her.

GIUSEPPE

Get out!

[Vattene!]

Ninetta doesn't move, Giuseppe throws the cloak on the floor, grabs Ninetta by the arm, and roughly pushes her away.

GIUSEPPE

Get out!

[Vattene!]

NINETTA

Defying him.

The goodness to leave! Goodness! You should thank me! Without me they'd have hung you.

[Solo sta grazia solo sta grazia, tu m'a a ringraziare, se non era per mia a stóra ti avevano già impiccato...]

GIUSEPPE

Firmly.

I don't want you to stay here, and that's final!

[Non voglio che resti qui, e basta!]

NINETTA

Shouting.

And you talk to me about goodness?

[...E mi parli pure di carità?]

GIUSEPPE

I won't listen to you any longer.

[Non ne voglio sentiri...]

NINETTA

Shouting, panting.

You have to deal with me, not your brother!

[Tu t'hai da fare i conti con mia non con to frate!]

GIUSEPPE

Trying to calm her.

Ninetta, enough!

[Ninetta! basta!]

NINETTA

Shouting and screaming.

Who ruined us? You!

[Perché tu n'arruvinasti! Tu!]

Giuseppe slaps her violently, slamming her against the wall. She collapses, then gets to her feet, sobbing.

NINETTA

In a murmur.

I'm staying, and you can't stop me.

[Io cca restu, niente puoi fare tu!]

Giuseppe lowers his head.

Front hall of Moschella's house.
Interior. Night.

The door opens. Ninetta steps in.

She slowly takes off her coat and hangs it on a peg. Salvatore, looking anxious, and dressed in his nightshirt, walks over to her.

SALVATORE

What happened?

[Cosa è successo?]

NINETTA

Nothing, nothing, just forget it.

[Niente, niente, non te ne incaricare.]

SALVATORE

But why did they keep you so long?

[Ma allora perché ti hanno tenuta tutto sto tempo?]

NINETTA

I'm telling you, everything's fine.

[Dissi che sta bono.]

SALVATORE

I don't understand.

[Non capisco.]

NINETTA

Curtly.

I'm tired, I don't feel like talking.

[Senti, sono stanca. Non ho voglia di parlarne.]

She turns and climbs the stairs.

SALVATORE

Greatly annoyed, yelling upstairs.

Don't forget, at eight a.m. tomorrow you have to be at the consulate to pick up your passport. For your information, signore Celi was kind enough to issue new tickets for us.

[Non dimenticare che domattina alle otto ci aspettano al consolato per il tuo passaporto. E poi ti informo che il signor Celi ha avuto la compiacenza di rifarci i biglietti.]

The door to Ninetta's room slams noisily.

Carmelo and Pasquale's room.
Interior. Night.

A bit later. We see Ninetta's silhouette approaching Carmelo's bed. Her coat is folded over her arm, and she's carrying a bag. She shakes Carmelo to wake him. He opens his eyes.

NINETTA

Excited, in a low voice.

Carmelo! Do you remember that place you told me about?

[Carmelo! Ti ricordi du postu chi mi dicisti?]

CARMELO

Half asleep.

Hmmm...?

NINETTA

That place you told me about! Did you forget?

[U postu che mi dicisti! Tu scordasti?]

CARMELO

No, no...

NINETTA

Take me there, quick!

[Portami là, subito!]

Carmelo, who is fully awake now, answers in a loud voice.

CARMELO

Now? What about the captain?

[Mo? E u capitano?]

NINETTA

Shh! He's sleeping. Hurry, for pity's sake!

[Chuuut! Sta dormendo. Andiamo dai, fammi stà misericordia.]

Carmelo, still under the covers, sits up in bed and points to his trousers, which are hanging over a chair.

CARMELO

My trousers.

[I pantaloni.]

Ninetta grabs the trousers and hands them to him. Carmelo takes them and looks at her without moving. Ninetta senses Carmelo's embarrassment, and walks toward the door, pulling on her coat.

Alleyway. Exterior. Night.

With the help of an iron bar, Carmelo is trying to pry open the door of a house. The door finally gives way. They go in.

Alphonse Lamoureux's store.
Interior. Night.

Carmelo and Ninetta enter a large, empty room. We recognize Alphonse's store. They take the stairs leading to the second floor.

Dining room in Félicité's apartment.
Interior. Night.

Ninetta is standing in the dining room. Carmelo appears in the doorway of Alphonse's old bedroom, and motions her to enter.

CARMELO

Come in, you'll be better off in here.

[Vinissi, qua dentro che è meglio.]

Alphonse's old bedroom. Interior. Night.

CARMELO

See, there's a mattress.

[Vardassi, c'è nu materassu.]

Ninetta puts her bag on a chair and immediately begins to settle in. Carmelo tries to untie the cord around the old rolled-up mattress.

NINETTA

Wait! You should go back. I'll do that.

[Aspetta! E megghiu chi tinni torni; m'arrangio io.]

CARMELO

No one will find you here. I promise!

He touches his cap.

I'll come back tomorrow.

[Qua dentro non vi trova niscuino. Parola mia! A domani.]

He disappears.

NINETTA

Till tomorrow, Carmelo.

[A domani, Carmelo.]

Ninetta stands there, her face filled with fear.

Moschella's workroom. Interior. Day.

Carmelo sits at the table, sewing. Behind him, Salvatore appears in a bathrobe; he glances around the workroom, perplexed.

SALVATORE

Carmelo, where's the signora?

[Carmelo, dov'è la signora?]

CARMELO

I don't know, I haven't seen her. Asleep maybe.

[Non lo so... Non l'ho vista... Forse dorme.]

Sceptical and annoyed, Salvatore goes upstairs. Carmelo watches him with a smile.

Upstairs hall of Moschella's house. Interior. Day.

Salvatore knocks on Ninetta's door.

SALVATORE

Ninetta... Ninetta, we have to go!

[Ninetta... Ninetta... dobbiamo andare!]

Receiving no answer, he decides to open the door, and sees that the room is empty.

SALVATORE

Where the devil can that damn woman be?

[Dove diavolo se n'è iuta, sta benedetta donna!]

He quickly goes back downstairs.

SALVATORE

Shouting.

Carmelo!!!

Alphonse's old bedroom in Félicité's apartment. Interior. Day.

A match is struck, and a candle is lit. Ninetta, who has dozed off, wakes with a start, frightened, then lets out a sigh of relief.

NINETTA

Ah! Carmelo!

Carmelo lights the candle on the dresser.

CARMELO

Proudly.

The captain called the police. They're searching for you everywhere. Celi even put a notice in the paper. Let them look. They'll never find you!

[U capitanu ha chiamato a police, vi stanno cercando a destra e a sinistra. Celi ha anche fatto mettere un annuncio sopra u giornale... hanno voglia di cercarvi! Qui non verranno mai!]

Carmelo sits down next to Ninetta and takes a sandwich wrapped in paper from inside his jacket. He offers her the sandwich.

NINETTA

Thank you, Carmelo.

[Grazie, Carmelo.]

Ninetta tears open the paper and bites into the sandwich hungrily. Carmelo removes his cap, crosses his arms, and watches Ninetta, grinning broadly.

CARMELO

You're hungry, eh?

[Tenete fame, eh!]

Without stopping, Ninetta vigorously nods 'yes'.

Alberto Celi's reception hall.
Interior. Night.

In a large, empty hall, a small table covered with a white tablecloth. Salvatore and Celi sit face to face, a bottle of champagne between them. Salvatore is wearing his uniform. He seems preoccupied.

CELI

Let's speak frankly, Comandante.

He stands up and moves his chair closer to Salvatore.

As long as you're here, that stubborn creature won't come out of hiding. She's making fools of us both. And our ball? I can't postpone it. How will I look? Listen... we've saved your brother. You've done your duty. Do as I suggest: take the boat the day after tomorrow. Go back to Italy in peace. That damn woman will come out of hiding and we can hold our celebration.

[Parliamoci chiaro, Comandante... Finché lei qui questa donna, cocciuta com'è, non esce allo scoperto... E ci tiene tutti in scacco! E la festa? Io non posso rimandarla da capo, che figura ci farei? Mi ascolti... Suo fratello, l'abbiamo salvato... Lei il suo dovere lo ha fatto... Facca come le dico io: prenda la nave dopodomani, se ne torni in Italia tranquillo, così questa santa donna esce fuori e noi potremo fare la festa ad honorem causa!]

We hear the opening bars of an aria from Rigoletto, sung by Caruso. Salvatore glances discreetly over his shoulder. Celi puts his arm on Salvatore's arm.

CELI

In a confidential tone.

Captain, I've arranged a little surprise for you. You won't be here for our celebration, but it will be better than the ball. I'll be right back!

[Capitano, ho preparato una surpresina per lei... Lei non ci sarà alla festa, ma questa serata sarà meglio della festa! Torno subito!]

He gets up and disappears. Salvatore turns around, puzzled.

Corridor leading to Celi's reception hall. Interior. Night.

Alida and Olivine, two gaudily dressed prostitutes, are waiting in the corridor. Alida smiles to Celi as he approaches.

CELI

Alida, flame of my heart!

ALIDA

To Olivine.

You see how gallant Alberto is!

CELI

And who is this lovely siren?

ALIDA

Olivine. I've told her all about you.

CELI

Unctuously.

A pleasure!

Celi kisses Olivine's hand. Alida glances curiously in Salvatore's direction. Celi offers them his arm.

CELI

Come along, my angels. A gentleman is waiting.

They walk toward Salvatore, who stands to greet them.

CELI

Comandante, Alida.

Salvatore bows and kisses her hand.

SALVATORE

Madame...

ALIDA

Sir...

Sacristy of the church in St. Zénon. Interior. Day.

Félicité is sitting on a bench next to Alphonse. Behind them the door of the confessional opens. A woman steps out and leaves. Father Phaneuf appears.

FATHER PHANEUF

Félicité!

Félicité gets up; after a few seconds Alphonse does too.

Monsieur Lamoureux!

The priest offers his hand.

What a surprise. We don't often have the pleasure of seeing you.

ALPHONSE

You know, Margie, my wife, in her condition, she needs my constant care.

FATHER PHANEUF

I understand... But she also takes good care of you, doesn't she?

The priest motions for them to sit down, then settles beside them, before going on.

FATHER PHANEUF

Has your daughter told you of my offer? So, Félicité, have you thought it over?

FÉLICITÉ

Yes, Father. I think it would be good for the children if you could arrange a place for them at the school in Valleyfield.

FATHER PHANEUF

They'll be very happy there, monsieur Lamoureux. It's an excellent school. And you, Félicité, you'll feel right at home here in the presbytery. You'll be earning your living while serving God at the same time. You've made the right decision. I knew you would!

Félicité takes a deep breath, as if to gather all her courage.

FÉLICITÉ

As for working, Father, I've decided to go back to Montreal. We put a lot of money into the store. I can't just let it go. I have to think of my future, and my children's. With them at school, I can make a new start. When school's out, they can come live with me. It'll be easier for me then.

FATHER PHANEUF

Standing up, angry.

You're asking me to be an accomplice to your damnation. I can't accept.

FÉLICITÉ

All I'm asking, Father, is a simple act of charity for my children.

ALPHONSE

Christian charity, Father.

FATHER PHANEUF

In the same tone.

Do you know what Christian charity is, monsieur Lamoureux? It's a two-edged sword. One must wield it with care.

To Félicité.

Go back to that jungle, if that's what you want. It has blinded you already, and you don't even realize it. Montreal is becoming a sewer that collects garbage from all over the world. All those foreigners acting as if they were in their own country, or even worse. And no one stops them.

To Alphonse, furious.

You should know. Look at how that murderer got off the hook.

Alphonse stands up.

A perfect example!

ALPHONSE

Containing his anger.

Father, Moschella was my friend, I knew him well. You have no idea what you're saying.

To Félicité.

Come along!

Félicité doesn't move.

I'll wait for you outside.

Alphonse leaves without saying goodbye to the priest.

FATHER PHANEUF

Your decision is final.

He puts his hand on Félicité's shoulder; she shudders.

But know that if the Lord should ever bring you back here, my door will always be open.

Félicité gets up.

FÉLICITÉ

Coldly, without turning around.

I'll manage, Father.

Presbytery veranda. Exterior. Day.

Félicité walks over to Alphonse, angry with him.

FÉLICITÉ

Curtly.

I suppose you're proud of yourself.

ALPHONSE

I can't allow someone to talk like that about my friends.

FÉLICITÉ

He's all you care about, your Italian. Théo's murderer!

ALPHONSE

That's not true!

FÉLICITÉ

If he'd been a French Canadian, he would've hung! Your money was well spent.

ALPHONSE

There's no point talking with you about it. Anyway, Moschella's my business.

FÉLICITÉ

And aren't I your business, too?

She descends the stairs.

ALPHONSE

Félicité!

Alphonse follows her to the carriage, where she is now seated.

ALPHONSE

Félicité... I'll keep the kids here with me. They'll be better off than with that bunch of hypocrites.

FÉLICITÉ

In a softer tone.

What about your invalid wife?

Alphonse climbs up beside her and takes the reins.

FÉLICITÉ

It would help if you could look after Rita. I'll take Léon to Montreal. He's old enough to help in the store.

Alphonse pats Félicité on the knee affectionately, and whips the horse. The carriage sets off.

Félicité's apartment. Interior. Night.

Hearing the sound of a carriage, Ninetta goes to the window in Alphonse's room. The carriage stops in front of the house.

Félicité's store. Interior. Night.

Through the store window, we see Félicité and Léon step down from a carriage. They enter, carrying their bags, and go upstairs. We see Carmelo's shadow, then Carmelo cautiously approaching the stairway.

Dining room in Félicité's house.
Interior. Night.

The light goes on. Félicité and Léon put down their bags.

LÉON

Removing his cap.

I'm thirsty.

He disappears. Félicité is slowly taking off her hat when she hears a door creak in the store downstairs. Félicité stops what she's doing and listens. Hearing nothing, she closes the door and puts away her hat. Suddenly, another sound, this time from Alphonse's old bedroom. Félicité walks slowly toward the door and opens it.

FÉLICITÉ

Incredulous.

What are you doing here?

In the dressing table mirror, we see the reflection of Ninetta, standing in the back of the room.

FÉLICITÉ

Yelling, enraged.

What are you doing here?

NINETTA

In a trembling voice.

I didn't do anything, madame. I didn't hurt your house.

FÉLICITÉ

Get out of here, now!

Terrified, Ninetta shakes her head 'no'. Félicité strides over to her.

FÉLICITÉ

Screaming, beside herself.

I said get out! Did you understand? Get out this minute!

Ninetta backs up against the wall. Félicité tries to drag her outside. Defending herself, Ninetta bites Félicité on the hand. She lets go with a yelp of pain.

FÉLICITÉ

Walking backward toward the door.

I'll get you out of here, you'll see!

She pushes Léon ahead of her, and they both disappear down the stairs.

Félicité's store. Interior. Night.

Félicité and Léon rush through the store and out into the street. Carmelo appears noiselessly, checks that Félicité has really left, then races up the stairs.

CARMELO

Signora! Signora, come on! The captain's left. He took the train to New York. Come on.

[Signora! Signora, venite! U Capitanu è partito; ha pigliato u trenu pi New York... Venite.]

Alphonse's old bedroom. Interior. Night.

In the darkness, Carmelo and Ninetta hastily gather her belongings.

CARMELO

Hurry, signora, the Frenchwoman will get the police!

[Forza, signora, prima cca 'a francisa torna cca police!]

NINETTA

Is there anyone outside?

[C'è gente fora?]

CARMELO

No, no. There's nobody in the street.

[Non, non... Sta nisciuno inta ruella!]

Carmelo and Ninetta hurry out of the room and down the stairs.

Félicité's store. Interior. Night.

Carmelo and Ninetta race toward the store's back door, which opens onto the alleyway. Ninetta stops.

NINETTA

Carmelo! I forgot my notebook!

[Carmelo! Mi scurdai u quadernu!]

She turns and starts back upstairs.

CARMELO

Signora!

He catches her by the arm and pulls her firmly with him.

There's no time, hurry! Come on, let's go!

[Amu a nesciri i'ccà... prestu! Forza... Iamu!]

Children's room, Félicité's apartment. Interior. Night.

The door opens. A policeman looks in silently, then returns to the kitchen next door, where Félicité is seated at the table. We hear steps off-camera, then another policeman appears.

SECOND POLICEMAN

You can lay charges, if you wish, madame, for breaking and entering.

FÉLICITÉ

No, there's no point.

SECOND POLICEMAN

As you wish. Good night, madame.

Félicité gets up to see them out.

Alphonse's old bedroom. Interior. Night.

Under the bed is Ninetta's notebook. Léon stoops to pick it up. He opens it and leafs through it before leaving the room.

Félicité's dining room. Interior. Night.

Félicité is sitting at the table. Léon comes in and hands her Ninetta's diary.

LÉON

Mom, look what I found.

Félicité leafs through it slowly. She seems moved by what she reads there.

Corridor leading to Celi's reception hall. Interior. Day.

Hustle and bustle in the corridor, which is decorated with banners in the colours of the Italian flag. Waiters carry platters laden with food and bottles of wine. Preparations for the ball are well underway. Celi appears agitated. He goes to the door leading to the hall.

CELI

Otello, quick!

[Otello! Vieni!]

Otello appears in the doorway. Celi leads him into the corridor.

CELI

Otello, it's time. I promised signora Moschella to pick her up from the prison at six.

[Otello, vai adesso, ho promesso alla signora Moschella che alle sei andavi a prenderla alla prigione.]

OTELLO

Obsequious.

At your orders, sir!

[Agli ordini, Cavaliere!]

He heads for the exit.

CELI

Yelling.

If she tries to back out, be firm with her. Remember!

[Se trova altre scuse insisti, eh! Mi raccomando!]

Otello leaves. A young delivery boy enters with a huge bouquet of red and white carnations.

CELI

Relieved.

Finally! This way, this way...

Celi accompanies him into the hall.

Prison waiting room. Interior. Day.

Seated on a bench, Ninetta patiently waits for Giuseppe to be brought in. The door to the room opens, and we see a guard murmur something to the guard watching the room. The latter goes to Ninetta.

GUARD

Madame? Please come with me.

At first, Ninetta is paralyzed with fear. Then she slowly gets up and walks out, followed by the guard.

Corridor leading to Celi's reception hall. Interior. Day.

Lively music shows that the ball is in full swing. Standing at the door, Celi welcomes his guests.

CELI

In English.

Signora, a pleasure! Come in.

Continuing in Italian.

Signora, what a pleasure! Come in! Maria, how are you? Ciao, Carlo!

[Signora, molto piacere! Avanti! Maria, come vai? Ciao, Carlo!]

Celi sees monsieur Leblanc, a reporter from La Patrie. *He opens his arms, goes to greet him, and shakes his hand.*

Monsieur Leblanc! How kind of you to accept my invitation!

He takes him by the arm and leads him toward the hall.

I so enjoyed your articles on poor Moschella. That's what I call journalism! If everyone wrote like you, we'd get along much better in this country.

LEBLANC

You're far too kind, monsieur Celi. Is madame Moschella here? I hoped to interview her later.

CELI

Of course! She'll be here any minute.

Celi sees Otello coming in.

CELI

There they are!

Celi takes a few steps toward Otello, who seems troubled.

Otello! Where's signora Moschella?

[Otello! E la signora Moschella?]

Otello glances at Leblanc, then whispers a few words in Celi's ear. Leblanc watches on, suspecting a problem. Celi appears stunned by the news he's heard. He walks to Leblanc.

Appalled.

He committed suicide!

LEBLANC

What?

CELI

Moschella! Yes, yes.

Calling on him as his witness.

You see how they are! That dirty lot!

Raising his voice.

How could anyone do such a thing?

Ungrateful swine! The bastard! And today of all days!

[Ingrati, ingrati! Sto disgraziato!]

OTELLO

Timidly.

What do we do now?

[E mo' che famo, sor Celi?]

CELI

What *can* we do? Tell them to go home! The party's over!

Otello walks toward the hall.

Snow-covered country road. Exterior. Day.

Ninetta and Pietro Fichera are driving slowly through the peaceful, snow-covered countryside.

PIETRO

This is my last winter here.

[Chista è l'ultima nivi chi mi vidu.]

NINETTA

Why?

[Picchi?]

PIETRO

Six years of Canada are enough. I'm going home. I bought a farm. Do you ever think of going back, signora?

[Sei anni di Canadà mi bastano... Me ne tornu... M'accatai una terra o paese. Signura non ci pensa di riturnarsini?]

Ninetta does not answer. A beat.

NINETTA

Please, stop for a minute, Pietro. I won't be long.

[Pietro, ni firmamu nu mumento. Haiu a fari na cosa.]

Pietro stops his horse. Ninetta looks at the countryside around her, then steps down from the wagon and takes a few steps in the snow. She walks over to some bushes, and squats to urinate. Standing up, she contemplates the countryside.

PIETRO

Yelling.

Signora, we should go!

[Signora, siamo pronti!]

Alphonse's house in St. Zénon.
Exterior. Day.

Ninetta and Pietro have climbed down from the wagon,
which is now in front of Alphonse's barn. Pietro, carrying a box
with the Sicilian puppets, and Ninetta walk toward the house. The
door opens, and Alphonse steps out.

NINETTA

'Yesterday the widow brought me my notebook. Too bad I
wasn't home. I'd like to have thanked her. Today I went to
visit monsieur Alphonse with the puppets that Giuseppe left
him. He was as happy as a child.'

['Ieri la mugghiera du morto mi portao u quaderno, peccato
che non ero a casa. L'avessi voluta ringraziare. Oggi sono
andata a trovare monsieur Alphonse per portarci i pupi che
Giuseppe ci ha lasciato. Era felice come un picciriddu.']

Façade of Alphonse's house.
Exterior. Night

We see light at one of the windows.

NINETTA

'All of a sudden it turned very cold. Monsieur Alphonse in-
sisted that we spend the night with him. I can't sleep here.
Tomorrow I return to Montreal. For now I have nothing
more to write.'

['Poi si mise a fare freddo forte. Monsieur Alphonse ha in-sistito e ci ha fatti rimanere nella sua casa per passare la notte. Ccà non posso dormire. Domani torno a Montreal. E ora non ho più niente da scrivere.']

Country fields. Exterior. Day.

Ninetta, dressed in black, is walking alone through the snow. Soon she will be nothing more than a distant figure contemplating the horizon.

The End

The Work of Paul Tana

Francesco Loriggio

The opening sequence of Paul Tana's film, *La Sarrasine*, shows a group of Italian immigrants who are watching a puppet show. On the improvised stage – we are inside a 'boarding house' in turn-of-the-century Montreal – Sicilian marionettes weave one of the tales they have become famous for. Passion and honour, war and sacrifice, religious and secular yearnings criss-cross, mingle and rapidly proceed toward their fated, inevitable climax. In this particular case, we are being presented with a dramatized version of an episode of Tasso's *La Gerusalemme liberata*. Tancredi, the Christian protagonist, has been fighting a surprisingly chivalrous and well-mannered Saracen champion. After a long battle, he has managed to inflict mortal wounds, but as he is is readying to dispense the baptism his opponent has entreated him to perform, he discovers to his dismay that he has actually killed his beloved Clorinda, the infidel woman whose favours he has been continuosly and desperately wooing.

The scene condenses many things. Spectators observing other spectators, we are given, at one remove, a very powerful example of the culture of emigration. The tone of the voice-over that in the film recites Tasso's Renaissance octaves leaves no room for mistakes: it is high poetry we are seeing and hearing, high poetry which the puppetry popularizes without condescension. Thus, the images stand for the strategy of the immigrant, who is dependent on high literary forms and adapts them to his or her own use. *La*

Sarrasine will tell its story against a backdrop as epic, as collective and grandiose as the one which, in Tasso's and other Renaissance romances, pitted Islamic against Christian characters, Western against Middle-Eastern or African mores. Like *La Gerusalemme liberata*, Tana's film will also attest to the centrality of the theme of the contact between cultures in Western fiction, but it will do so in a different tone. Put side by side with the stylized recitation, the carefully pronounced Italian of the verses, the 'dialectophone', street-language-responses of the spectators preempt, situate the plot that is to come. The characters of the puppet show are inscribed in the memory of the emigrants — a memory sufficiently generalized to cancel out its sources, to be almost anonymous: how many of the spectators realize that the verses come from Tasso? — but the emigrants cannot be like Tancredi or Clorinda. Part of the point of the scene is to let us know that in emigration there can be no larger-than-life figures, that the proper realm of modern contact is history, a realm which yields clichés, or at best types and even stereotypes, not heroes and heroines, chivalrous or otherwise.

The scene serves an important structural function: it prefigures and then helps to underscore a lot that happens in the film. For *La Sarrasine*, a title which could be translated as The Saracen Woman, is also about about men and women, about the way cultural and sexual relations — cultural and sexual politics — unfold in Canada, in our own century. Tana begins by recounting the events preceding, leading to and following the controversial murder of a Montreal businessman by an Italian tailor. For a good portion of the film, the action focusses on the efforts by him, his wife and his and friends to appeal the trial and to have his death sentence commuted. Then, slowly, almost unawarely, the attention shifts to the wife – how she fights for her husband's cause, how she learns to read and to write, how she resists the attempts of her husband's relatives to convince her to return to Italy. By the end of the film, the woman, alone, but more determined than ever to remain in Canada, has become the true protagonist of the story.

Immigrants – their roles vis-à-vis each other and their place in the affairs of this country – have always been a major theme of Paul Tana's work. His first feature-lengt film, *Les grands enfants* (1980), appeared at the height of the nationalist wave of the seventies, had Montreal as its background, and highlighted characters who spoke only Portuguese or who could alternate between English and French at will or who were of Italian origin. His second film, *Caffè Italia* (1985), records, docu-drama style, the presence of the Italian community in Montreal from the early decades of the century to the eighties. Indeed, while three films don't really constitute a full-fledged filmography, it is clear that Tana is, so far, the only Canadian director who has dealt seriously with immigration. Even when they are not the main characters, the Italian-Canadians in his films are not there just to provide local colour, the occasion for easy effect; they and the issues that go with emigration are the material by which he says what it is he has to say.

In this regard, the most immediately striking feature of Tana's cinema is its undivided commitment to the two dimensions of the stories it narrates. To put immigrants on screen is, in his films, to retell from a different perspective that which has been told over and over, to update and to refurbish the images about this country by peopling them with characters until now left out of the picture. Whether events are located in the present or in the past, story is, for Tana, inseparable from history, and vice versa. In short, the filmmaker is a revisionist, the purveyor of counter-memories or counter-fictions, and the explorer of the tensions between the collective and the private levels of life.

Not by coincidence, Tana has co-scripted his last two works, *Caffè Italia* and *La Sarrasine*, with Bruno Ramirez, who is a professional historian and the author of several books about Italian-Canadian and Italian-American communities, besides being himself an immigrant. In this respect, too, the circumstances are, I believe, unique in Canadian cinema. I spoke about such matters and about *La Sarrasine* with Tana and Ramirez a few weeks before the film's official release.

Francesco Loriggio: The cast of *La Sarrasine* includes various Italian actresses and actors. Is it a co-production?

Paul Tana: No, it's produced by the Association coopérative de productions audiovisuelles (ACPAV), here in Montreal. It could have easily been a co-production. Together with such Canadian actors as Tony Nardi and Jean Lapointe, we were lucky to have Enrica Maria Modugno, whom you may remember from the Taviani brothers' *Night of the Shooting Stars* and *Kaos* or from Nanni Moretti's *La messa è finita*, as well as Gaetano Cimarosa (he was in Brusati's *Bread and Chocolate*) and Biagio Pelligra, both well-known in Italy. But the world of producers in Italy is a very complicated one and we didn't insist.

F.L.: You've completed the subtitling of the dialogue parts of *La Sarrasine* which are in Italian or in Sicilian. The re-recording is also finished. In the private showing I attended, the reaction of the spectators was good. What is the schedule for the film now?

P.T. Distribution in Montreal and Quebec theatres will begin on February 22. We still have to subtitle the film in English. Hopefully, some sort of distribution outside Quebec will be possible for the fall of 1992. Before then, however, and in fact even before it starts circulating in any public theatres, the film will appear at the Rendez-vous du cinema Quebecois, a week devoted entirely to the year's productions in Quebec. *La Sarrasine* will close the Rendez-vous. I am also happy to announce that our film has been selected to go to the Berlin Festival, an important event in the year's round of cinematic meetings. The film will appear simultaneously at the Rendez-vous and at Berlin. On more or less the same day, around February 15th, I believe.

F.L. The Rendez-vous turned out to be an excellent, very propitious launching ground for your previous film, *Caffè Italia*, since it was named best Quebec film of the year. On the other hand, the atmosphere in Quebec seems to have changed somewhat since then. There seems to be less enthusiasm for ventures that dwell too much on the plurality of Quebecois society. The idea of multiculturalism itself is met with a growing impatience. Does this worry you? Has this change of climate had any effect on the writing and/or shooting of your film?

P.T. No, I can't say that the question of the fit with the spirit of the times really worried us. Personally I'm not persuaded the change you mention has taken place. But, you know, we're going to publish the script of *La Sarrasine*, and in the preface we indicate very clearly what our main problem was. Our problem — and our first concern — was how to tell, how to narrate the story we had in mind. Obviously, in writing this script, and then in shooting the film, we took certain positions. We did so rather explicitly and very deliberately. Those views may not please some people, but, to repeat, our main preoccupation was how to express our story, how to be faithful to it.

F.L.: The reason I asked the question is this: in your film *Les grands enfants* characters don't hide their ethnic identity, but they assume it almost without realizing it, without awareness. Identity is not the main theme of the film. *Caffè Italia*, instead, is about *italianità* in Montreal. It's the story of the community, and, as such, a consciousness-raising exercise. Characters think about themselves, and they do it by seeing themselves in relation to the community or to its history. In *La Sarrasine*, the characters know who they are, socially, but they are more interested in addressing their own individual problems. The film doesn't endeavour to establish direct links between the protagonists and the Italian immigrant community. Not only that, it hinges primarily on the development of one character. Most of the action is situated inside; an air of intimacy, privacy hovers over the story after a while.

P.T.: Yes, there is intimacy, privacy, especially after the murder. The film is ultimately about Ninetta, the woman who,

faced with the imprisonment of her husband, has to con-
struct her future. In our first versions of the script, we had
included various scenes that depicted the Montreal of the
turn-of-the-century, and the Italian immigrant community
at large. Our original idea was that of a film which was also
an epic film. An epic film and a much more expensive film.
Except that writing is not the same as shooting. When you're
writing, money is not a consideration. It often becomes the
primary criterion during shooting: you have to do the best
you can with the budget you have. It's the way it is with
cinema. That said, I don't think *La Sarrasine*, as it is, stresses
the private dimension at the expense of the other, the collective. It simply shows the collective unepically.

For example, in the very last scene Ninetta goes out
into the wide open space – miles and miles of snow. It's an
image anticipated a couple of scenes before when she gets off
the cart in which she is traveling walks into the landscapes,
squats down and urinates. For both of these images we re-
ceived quite a bit of criticism at the shooting and editing
stage. Perhaps they're too lyrical, both of them. But there
they are: the protagonist of the film, wearing black, the dress
we associate not only with widowed women but with Italian
– and particularly Southern Italian – women, finally con-
fronts the landscape. Her gesture is a choice, or – better –
an appropriation. She is saying: 'This now is also my land.'
Yet she does what she does as a Sicilian, carrying all her past
with her. The black she is wearing doesn't mourn just the
death of her husband. It's the colour of a condition; it be-
speaks the manner in which many people have participated
– and still participate – in the making of this country. For
me these images are a statement about the collective dimen-

sion, or, if you will, a political statement. As the camera draws back, the Sicilian widow is a black spot on the endless white of the background. But impurity is at the heart of this country, whether nationalists — of whatever stripe — like it or not.

F.L.: And, of course, Ninetta is a woman in a story that had begun as a story of men...

Bruno Ramirez: Yes, this is very important. At a certain moment, we realized that we were trying to follow too many characters. We didn't have the budget for either a long or a crowded film, but it finally occurred to us that we had in Ninetta a character who brought together and recapitulated all the strands of the story rather neatly. She goes through processes of personal growth — she learns to write, starts keeping a diary, takes hold of her life — but she is also — by the very fact that she is a woman and a wife in a Southern Italian family — entangled in a number of other conflicts. She has to struggle against the authority of her brother-in-law just arrived from Italy, who wants her to board the next ship home; she has to fend off the eloquence of an Italian *notabile*, a self-appointed community leader, who espouses her husband's cause for his own purposes. When we look back now, we think we would have chosen that route even if we had had more money. The collective comes into the images of the film via representative figures, via individuals and the institutions they stand for — a judge, a policeman, a husband, a brother-in-law, a community leader who likes to make speeches, etcetera. Ninetta's story is by itself, as a story, intrinsically political. Narrating those politics was enough for us. We didn't need to worry about the run of affairs around us.

This is why when we're asked if we tried to make a feminist film, we answer that, although the characters and their actions may be interpreted in that sense, we didn't impose on them a feminist ideology. In her own fashion — she is unlettered, she expresses herself in very basic terms — Ninetta reaches quite a heightened degree of awareness. Once she understands what has been happening to her and around her, she accepts no nonsense from anybody. But she never stops being a wife. She explains to her jailed husband that their relationship cannot be what it was before, but she continues to love him. You could even say that she develops a deeper solidarity with him now that she realizes how free she can be.

F.L: Does she, then, relate to him also as a person, in the end? Is emigration the process which, when successful, as in the case of Ninetta, leads to the solidarity you speak of, a solidarity on the level of the person?

B.R.: I suppose we could say, using big words, that emigration can have a liberating, emancipatory function. To decide to emigrate, you know very well, is already to cut some bonds, to attempt an escape. And settling in another country encourages self-reflection, hence the rise of a social consciousness. This is the side of emigration that best attests to its modernity. Obviously, caveats have to be added. In our film and in real life, not all immigrants are like Ninetta. There is, for example, the organ-player, who moves about from town to town, who never settles, and who lives and experiences emigration more or less along traditional lines.

There is again the *notabile*, the very rhetorical, lawyer-community leader, who seizes the occasion to put himself on a pedestal and acts as if he actually spoke for the Italian immigrants in Montreal or for 'Italianhood' as such. With Ninetta we see the emergence of different attitudes. We see emerging the immigrant as individual, as person, or what we might call the more progressive side of emigration.

P.T.: For me the last scene of the film can serve as an illustration here, too. When Ninetta goes out on the snow, her gesture is the gesture of an individual and the gesture of an individual who is an immigrant. A person is a sum of specific identities, after all, not an abstract entity. An individual is always complex, never simple. He or she is an impurity, a mixture. Ninetta is a woman and a wife, someone who wants to stay here in Canada and someone who mourns the past. I don't know if that's what you mean by person.

F.L.: *La Sarrasine* explores this aspect of emigration also in terms of its impact on the non-immigrants, on the host society. The wife of the Quebecois man whom Ninetta's husband kills comes to understand Ninetta's plight and feel some sympathy for her.

P.T.: Yes, Quebecois society is the mirror image of the immigrant society. It, too, harbours various degrees of social awareness.

F.L. I'd like to pursue this a bit further. Your film traces the coming to self-awareness of the main character, an awareness that coincides with the decision to stay in Canada, the acceptance, if you wish, of the hereness of Canada and the rest, including the mourning of the separation that the acceptance entails. To this extent, the film follows the route of

most narratives that have to do with first-generation immigrants: it is a film with a plot structured like a *Bildungsroman*,
a story about the 'education' of a character, who, as all first-
generation immigrants, 'discovers' Canada and places himself in relation to that discovery. We could already here
make some distinctions with stories about second- or third-
generation immigrants, whose 'education', on the contrary,
often leads to the re-discovery of the ethnic past. But that is
not my point. What follows self-awareness? How do we use
it? In your film some of the Quebecois characters (the wife
and the father-in-law of the murdered man) achieve a corre-
sponding level of understanding. Are we to make anything
of this? Is it an indication of the kind of society that might
be possible in Quebec? And the fact that the characters understand but are not able to go beyond understanding, does
it mean that the society that might be possible cannot yet be
narrated, is not yet tellable or showable?

B.R. I hope not many other people will ask us to answer
questions like that! Self-awareness, once it's there, works on
you. It's part of your mental universe, and you can't get away
from it: it will impinge on whatever you do, whether you're
an artist, a professor, a businessman or a businesswoman. At
any rate, a film is a film because it allows many types of
viewing. The one you propose is only one of them, not one
that I would necessarily resist, but only one of them. Don't
forget that ours is an historical film. We are narrating a story
about mass emigration as it occurred during the early decades the century, an emigration quite different from today's.
La Sarrasine narrates why we are what we are today as Mon-
trealers. The history of Montreal is also the history of private
dramas such as Ninetta has to endure.

P.T.: I would have to agree with Bruno that we have to start with the film as film, as an object that solicits questions — or answers for that matter — rather than give them. I would add one thing: even if the film is an historical film, it cannot avoid being contemporary. And Ninetta, that black dot on the Canadian whiteness, does offer a different image of Quebec than the one we are generally presented with, which has at its core references to the ethnic purity of the province. Immigrants aren't just there, parked in some back street. They participate actively — and have participated actively, since way back — in the landscape. In the film, the priest is perhaps the best incarnation of the ideology of purism. And perhaps the priest is one of Ninetta's more direct antagonists. We are here, even if — it seems — many fail to notice.

F.L.: In your film neither the murder of the Quebecois man nor the suicide of the Italian tailor are shown on screen. Are there any reasons for this reticence?

P.T.: With the Quebecois man the reasons are just narrative. By the time we started shooting we had come to the conclusion that our film was about Ninetta, and that events had to be seen from her perspective, or at least narrated in a way that would not detract from her centrality. As for the tailor, there was a technical problem, that we now refer to as the problem of blood. The script did call for us to show the dead tailor but we couldn't make the blood stains look realistic enough. We felt nobody would believe that those big red blobs were blood. They looked more like patches of molasses. So, although in this case we wanted to at least show the dead man, we decided not to.

F.L.: Let's move on to the future then. What projects are keeping you busy?

P.T.: Right now we are writing the script of a film entitled, tentatively, in English, *The Dream of Joe Aiello*. It's a story suggested to us by one of the Italian immigrants we interviewed while preparing *Caffè Italia* and which we kept out of that film. This man, who came to Canada with nothing and now owns a very successful business, asked us one day if we could do a film about his life. He wanted to leave something about himself to his children and grandchildren. We couldn't do that film, but the idea stuck with us and we worked on it until we got what I think is a very interesting script out of it.

F.L.: You're staying, then, with 'Italian' topics.

P.T.: Yes, of course, but I don't know if the adjective 'Italian' is appropriate, as a term. It's too stark, too simple. I can't tell you much more about Joe Aiello, other than to say that it'll be about the racism of minorities – all minorities. But for me that's the aim and aspiration of every director – to make something that is universal.

F.L.: Still, don't you think that the moment you choose to work with immigrant themes – and therefore themes pertaining to a minority or to minorities – you are willy-nilly obliged to minister to and possibly stress the cultural identity of your characters? That their identity is also – whether you want it or not – one of the issues of your story? The identity of majorities is hardly ever in question. Majority groups certainly don't question it.

P.T.: Perhaps in a story about immigrants the material is collective in various degrees and fashions. For me identity is connected with the desire of groups not to disappear, not to die. And this is universal. It is a desire majorities know as well as minorities. Look at recent Canadian history, though we could take our pick from many other nations. Majority groups also refuse to change, fight what brings change.

F.L.: Or, phrased differently, to be in the world today is really — as it used to be said here in Canada — to try to survive...

P.T.: More or less. What else is there? But to return to your question about our future. Other projects are gurgling in our mind for which we have yet no financing. On this, Bruno and I disagree. I don't believe *Joe Aiello* is the third film in the trilogy. We need another film to complete the threesome. For me *Caffè Italia* is something else, something like a mythology, or, more precisely, a foundation myth. It's a gold mine of potential scripts. We'll probably find in it another story, and go with the characters as they emerge. Ninetta has taught us that they know best.